THE LEADERSHIP PIN CODE

THE

LEADERSHIP

PIN CODE

* * *

Unlocking the Key to Willing
and Winning Relationships

DR NASHATER DEU SOLHEIM

LIONCREST
PUBLISHING

THE LEADERSHIP PIN CODE

Unlocking the Key to Willing and Winning Relationships

ISBN   978-1-5445-0718-7   *Hardcover*

978-1-5445-0716-3   *Paperback*

978-1-5445-0717-0   *Ebook*

978-1-5445-0719-4   *Audiobook*

To my wonderful son, you inspire me to be better in every way.

To my greatest teachers and leaders—my mum and dad for your empathy and unconditional kindness, humility and unwavering selflessness. Your legacy is captured in my heart.

CONTENTS

INTRODUCTION 9

1. THE DYSFUNCTIONAL BELIEFS OF LEADERS 27

2. CLOSE THE GAP 57

3. A IS FOR APPROACH AND ADVANCED PREPARATION...83

4. B IS FOR BODY LANGUAGE AND BEHAVIOUR............ 117

5. C IS FOR CONVERSATION 153

6. BRINGING IT ALL TOGETHER 197

CONCLUSION...................................... 225

ACKNOWLEDGEMENTS 229

ABOUT THE AUTHOR 233

INTRODUCTION

Stop for a minute now and answer this—when did you last pause to reflect on how you can be more effective as a leader?

In my experience, leaders take one of two approaches to improvement. There are those who are enlightened and proactive in their approach—let's say they 'pro-flect' rather than 're-flect'—and take the time to purposefully consider what they can do to become a more effective leader going forward.

And then there are those who are struggling—who are more *re*active than *pro*active. They try to get by in spite of this, reflecting only after the event on what they should have done or can do next time or when things go wrong.

In my experience, the latter is more common.

How often have you seen a leader march into a meeting, full of confidence and bravado, only to observe that he's unprepared? How often have you seen a leader simply winging it? Perhaps, like watching an actor give a poor performance on the stage, you may even feel sorry for him and cringe a little as he tries to communicate his message.

If only he had done a little more homework and put a little more thought into learning about his audience. If only he'd made eye contact rather than staring at his slides on the screen. If only he'd known how to communicate his message, the meeting could have been much more effective and even inspiring.

Ineffective preparation, along with misplaced behaviours and words, can be deal-breakers for a leader who's trying to engage an individual or a room full of people. It's obvious to everyone in the room (except perhaps the leader) that he's caught up in his own head and his own agenda. The frustration, of course, is that the audience who depends on that message won't get what they need in order to do what they're supposed to do. Instead of accepting responsibility, the leader inevitably complains that his audience didn't listen, didn't understand the key issues, or was simply incompetent. What he is experiencing is the all too familiar 'intention-impact' gap—he intended to communicate effectively with perhaps the best will in the world, but it failed to have the impact he wanted. He is left feeling frustrated and misunderstood.

Leaders today struggle with ever-changing challenges, demands and contexts to their roles. They may have strong influence in one area but fall short in another. The context in which you're leading at any moment is key to what you do or how you adapt your leadership style. Consider how you lead in the following contexts. How satisfied do you feel with the results you achieve and how would you like to improve? In chapter six, I'll give you concrete examples of how to navigate each of the following types of situations.

- Collaborative meetings and team working: Who talks the most in your meetings? If it's you as the leader, you need to ask yourself why you have a team. Having a disciplined approach that gives space to others before yourself is a good start. Managing meetings to achieve their purpose depends on what you need to achieve as a team and ensuring that it is clear from the outset.
- Dealing with unlikeable people: Do you like everyone you work with? Let's be honest, it's impossible to like everyone. There are some people with whom we get along and have an easy rapport and some we find trickier—or actually dislike. Leaders face the same challenges as anyone else, and they often acquire

team members or colleagues as part of their new role. In spite of any dislikes, whether they be due to conflicting personalities, values, interests, or habits, leaders have to find a way of working effectively with or towards those people anyway.

- Empowering your team: Are you challenged by prioritising your tasks, resources and time? And when it comes to helping others to do that for themselves, it is an added challenge. Leaders often have team members or peers who pass them monkeys, i.e., pass on problems or tasks they should either resolve themselves or identify possible solutions that the leader can then help select best options from. Leaders who train others on how to manage their own monkeys, so to speak, create more time and space for handling their own priorities whilst empowering others.

- Selling a business case or looking for buy-ins from stakeholders: How can you increase your chances of winning support? Having to position an idea you feel is necessary for your daily work or the future of the business is not as easy as it may sound. Competing priorities for investment and resources mean that even the best ideas may be left on the cutting room floor—there is a time for everything, as a CEO once told me.

- Difficult conversations: What are the rules of engagement that experienced mediators use to overcome or neutralise conflicts? From minor disagreements, pushback, and resistance to full-blown arguments and battles, leaders deal with conflictual situations frequently. In some cases, these are minor irritations that can be resolved quickly without much intervention. Other times, the leader is either in the centre himself or finds himself as a mediator between others in difficult conversations.

· Leading change: How do you secure acceptance, commitment and loyalty to a change in the organisation? Leaders handle many varied changes at all levels—from daily operations to reorganisations and mergers or acquisitions. Most organisations will say they're in a constant state of change, whether it's changing systems, policies, procedures, onboarding new team members, changing strategic direction or business priorities and reorganising or downsizing.

Experienced leaders are not immune to these same struggles, albeit in different contexts, such as lateral leadership engagement—i.e., collaboration with same-level peers on company-wide projects, achieving alignment with their senior stakeholders, managing transitions in mergers and acquisitions, splitting of businesses or introducing new business ideas or product lines. Their own teams, in spite of seniority or experience, may lose their strategic perspective and get lost in the details, or show resistance towards big organisational changes. Most frequent challenges are in the silos where people aren't working towards the common goals of the organisation, but rather for their own priorities. These leaders may even struggle to utilise the networks necessary for building alliances, cooperation, or support, or for learning from others' efforts in the same challenges, thereby unnecessarily reinventing wheels, or simply not seeking expert advice. They may have a thousand connections on LinkedIn, but don't manage to extract the value of those relationships in reality.

Leaders are presenting all the time: anything from presenting at the Monday meeting to their team, to leading town hall meetings, giving the goodbye speech at an employee's leaving event, or a keynote conference address. Yet, an inability to effectively translate their agenda and ideas in such a way that others feel engaged and mobilised by what they mean lies at the root of a leader's struggles. It's make-or-break on whether the leader is memorable for the right or wrong reasons. The leader's impact depends very much on preparation and delivery.

A leader's skill level and style tend to fall along a continuum from the least effective—what I consider the *entitled leader*—to the most effective—which I call the *engaged leader*. This isn't a case of either–or; depending on the context, your knowledge and skills, your position on the continuum likely fluctuates.

ENTITLED OR ENGAGED LEADER?

Let's first look at the characteristics of the leader at the *entitled* end of the continuum. This person is often recognisable as a newly appointed leader who upon coming into the role, sees a number of things to be improved upon or changed immediately. He approaches the situation with the mindset of 'My position grants me authority, power and mandate, and I'm just going to make the changes I see fit.' The changes may be as drastic as rewriting the company strategy, changing company goals, priorities, and organisation structure or as seemingly simple as changing the way meetings are run. Regardless of the type of changes, decisions are made and presented to the team as a *fait accompli*, without any attempt to gain buy-in or support from the team, nor to explain the rationale behind the changes. No time is spent getting to know the organisation or testing the ideas to make sure they're necessary or valid. Changes have no anchor within the organisation, nor from stakeholders. The changes are about the leader and their power to act, rather than mobilising the organisation.

The entitled leader seizes all ownership from the team, and as a result, people quickly disengage, becoming fearful and mistrustful of leadership. The leader is seen as unpredictable, impulsive and autocratic. The sense of instability as the culture changes for the worse causes people to worry that, at best, their tasks may change or they are no longer valued or, at worst, they'll lose their job. Because of the mistrust and lack of cooperation, attrition will increase as people move on to a place where they feel listened to and valued rather than continuing to work at the mercy of the entitled leader.

At the opposite end of the continuum sits an *engaged leader*. When placed in a new position of leadership, the engaged leader harnesses as much information as possible about the organisation, the culture, the teams and the individuals. He seeks input and buy-in from the team and tests changes to make sure they're relevant and necessary. He explains the motives for change, and because the team understands why the leader wants change, they become ambassadors of change *acceptance* to the rest of the organisation. The engaged leader is curious to find out who holds the information he needs to know and understands that the real influencers in the organisation may not be the ones with the formal mandates or grand titles. He knows how to best handle dialogues with individual team members or key stakeholders to establish rapport, build alliances and navigate the various parts of the organisation. He is politically savvy, as I call it.

The engaged leader harnesses input, not to achieve consensus, but to make sure those who need to be involved in decision making are involved, their ideas are valued, and feedback travels both ways. He is curious about where resistance lies and how his decisions will affect others. As such, he builds trust through respectful dialogue with the team and the effect is that people in the organisation rally together and collaborate even when bad news is shared. People will stay with the organisation because they feel involved and valued. Even if their ideas don't make the final cut, they feel party to and understand the basis for any big changes, especially when related to their tasks and priorities.

A well-known adage states, 'Tact is the ability to tell someone to go to hell in such a way that they look forward to the trip.'

Leadership is not about you as a leader, but about how you lead others. It's about the interests of the other party and how you can meet those interests whilst meeting your own and of course that of the business so that you both walk away with something valuable.

The leader holds a privileged position. Both the entitled leader and the engaged leader have mandate, authority and power, but they use them differently. The engaged leader garners the best possible cooperation and collaboration for the exact same changes the entitled leader imposes by force. On occasion, the engaged leader may be viewed as fearful or procrastinating yet is neither; he is setting himself—and the organisation—up for sustainable success and robustness in handling inevitable future changes.

Simply put—having been chosen or appointed to lead, the leader owes it to his audience to be more effective in his impact so that they can get what they need, and the leader doesn't have to work twice as hard to engage them.

He owes it to them to be an engaged leader.

Some people do have these natural leadership skills where we see they tend to be followed in spite of those around them feeling obliged contractually to do so. They have high-performing teams and respectful, cooperative, collegiate rules of engagement. These leaders have also built trust so deeply within their teams that they can challenge, handle conflict and differences of opinion, and use them to renew their agenda, goals and targets in a positive way—all whilst the relationships remain solid and intact.

These people are recognised as great leaders, but rarely does anyone unlock the key to how they lead with such ease of influence—until now. These leaders innately know what I call their PIN Code—understanding and being skilled at value-creating and relationship building through persuasion, influence and negotiation skills—yet they may not be conscious of how they use these skills.

This book will show you how.

PERSUADE, INFLUENCE, NEGOTIATE = PIN

As a leader, have you ever wondered why sometimes you get the traction you want with people and other times you don't? It's not luck—you must be able to persuade and influence those you lead to get results in a positive way, and the challenge is that everyone is different—right? Finding the win-win is critical to making this happen. Your team and key stakeholders must be willing to go in the direction you're asking them to go.

In my experience as a leader and working with leadership development, however, I observe leaders' frustration with their inability to get traction and engagement consistently. There's a gap or a missing link between what they know they need to do and how they get that message across. Leaders struggle with this gap every day—how do I persuade, influence and negotiate with my team and stakeholders?

Filling that gap is about learning PIN skills and training a set of muscles. Having worked as a front line leader and an executive leader in both small local and large international businesses, I realised how relevant many of these skills are to all leaders in their work with influencing and motivating teams, dealing with conflicts and trying to win over others to support their cases or agendas.

Chances are as an experienced leader you've attended multiple lengthy leadership or communication training workshops. Rather than getting caught in the same trap of long, protracted programs, I knew my method had to be intuitively useful, simple and pragmatic. It had to be something that leaders could remember easily and use in any moment effectively. I've thus developed a no-nonsense and unique method for training these muscles, building on my expertise and long experience in clinical psychology, business strategy and corporate leadership.

The PIN Code is about finding the hook—the interest and motivation—of the other person for creating a willing and winning relationship that delivers the results the business needs with you in the lead. If you've ever wondered how a psychologist encourages people to open up and commit to positive change, I'm going to show you how it's done with three keys. My psychological approach to leadership draws from my cross-cultural business experience and background as a clinical psychologist specialising in forensic and neuropsychology. Specifically, in neuropsychology working with brain injuries, I learned how to train the brain to learn new skills and change old patterns of behaviours. Then as a forensic clinical psychologist, I learned investigation and persuasion questioning techniques working with dangerous and mainly change-resistant offenders. These psychological techniques underlie the method I share with you in this book.

If you seek a memorable and pragmatic approach, I'm sure it will resonate with you as it has with many of my clients. I've developed a simple but impactful, common sense, easy-to-use method that exercises the PIN muscles. No long lectures or PowerPoint seminars, but rather an ABC method of approach (A) to behaviour (B) and conversation (C) that, once tried, leaves a memorable impact. If PIN is what you want to do, ABC is how you do it.

There are thousands of great leadership books and development programs, albeit some are complicated, lengthy and expensive. This book is not about replacing them but about crystallising how you use your knowledge—the what—in your everyday leadership to have the impact you want and need to have. From a one-minute conversation to a yearlong project, it provides the necessary method to implement everything business books tell you to do. And, it's more effective than complex academic literature telling you all the things you should know—simply because you'll remember how to use it.

THE RULE OF THREE

In working with leaders, I often heard that it was difficult to recall, never mind utilise, everything they learned on development programs, which were frequently several months, if not years, long. Books on the subject were informative but suffered from the same memory burden of too much information to be easily recalled and applied in daily reality. Having worked in the field of neuropsychology earlier in my career, I knew about effective learning strategies, the secret of the 'rule of three,' and how chunking of information eases recall. What neuroscience tells us is that humans tend to better remember—and quickly recall—information when it's chunked into three or four items. If you take a closer look, you'll notice that for the same reason, the rule of three is widely used in marketing: three bullets in a tagline, three ideas, or three images. They want you to remember them, and they've mastered the simple trick.

I knew if I was to create a guideline for leaders, I would need it to be memorable and easy to use—take my own medicine, so to speak. So, I too, borrowed the rule of three in creating a simple, usable framework but with content that had the integrity of PIN and explained in plain English—no buzz words, consultant speak, or academic jargon. No long lectures or PowerPoint seminars, the methodology is straightforward and effective. It's supported by sound research, theory and evidence-based practise from the fields of psychology and business. I offer an unforgettable way of having the impact and influence you need in your daily work. It's as simple as ABC.

- A = Approach: your mindset, your research into people, context, how you prepare for individual encounters or meetings by taking the time to learn about their interests, culture, or goals

- B = Behaviour: the physical behaviour and manner you use when meeting with people, including body language, choosing the right arena for the encounter, and how you set up a room or manage virtual meetings

- C = Conversation: the questions you ask, responses you give, and how you steer the conversation and dialogue, managing resistance and conflict, building trust

In your own interactions with others, you are likely doing all these things but are you aware of how you're doing them? Are you intentional and purposeful in communicating your agenda? Do you convey your needs, beliefs and priorities in a way that others are willing to join you easily? When leaders take the time to plan their approach, they'll behave skilfully, harnessing support whilst their conversations will secure their influence.

It comes down to learning the skill of translating the 'what' and 'why' to your team, partners and stakeholders—what you need to know about your business—your role, your responsibilities, your mandate and your tasks—and why you need to do those things.

The steps outlined in this book provide the keys to how.

First, you'll read about the dysfunctional beliefs that trip leaders up in their everyday work of leadership, so you can be sure to avoid them. Then, persuasion, influence, and negotiation (PIN approach, which are the skills you need to learn) are explained, followed by chapters dedicated to approach, behaviour and conversation (ABC) so that you'll leave with the tools that you can use to implement changes immediately. Throughout, I'll provide real-world examples from my experience with names and places changed to protect identities. You'll also find sidebars titled 'Dig Deeper' that point you in the direction to learn more about the theory and science behind the ideas I present.

BEFORE WE BEGIN, A CLARIFICATION

I often am asked whether this methodology I propose teaches people to be manipulative. In truth, humans manipulate every day, in many scenarios. We are all at some level, meeting our needs through how we develop relationships with others.

The difference boils down to intention and method.

The objective of my method is to create win-win situations, to influence and persuade so that you meet your needs whilst the person whom you're dealing with meets theirs. It's not about always compromising, i.e., coming away with less than you're happy with or giving in, nor about meeting your needs at the sole cost of theirs or by negating yours.

It's natural that we try as humans to create an impression to achieve the effect we want, and that is nevertheless authentic. Sometimes we have to fake it until we make it, but impression management is a struggle for the leader who gives away that his intention is to exploit someone else whilst offering superficial charm. In other words, he is giving off a false impression.

In business, entitled leaders are focused on driving their own agenda and are not interested in the consequences to the other party. Their impression management will be selfish, and even if not immediately noticeable, their team will soon come to realise they are pawns in the leader's bigger picture—you are there to serve their wins.

The engaged leader is successful in building purposeful connections with authentic intention, driven by curiosity and empathy. If you're a curious leader, this book will help you have the impact you want every day and preserve relationships with others whilst delivering exceptional results. It's about getting the best out of both, not at the cost of, or in spite of, somebody else.

By learning the method in the following pages, you can

positively change the effectiveness of your leadership immediately. Once you know your PIN Code, you will become the impactful leader you need to be.

Let's begin.

CHAPTER 1

* * *

THE DYSFUNCTIONAL BELIEFS OF LEADERS

'I'm leaving.'

Pierre said those words to Bill, his leader, over the phone one day after several failed attempts to schedule an appointment with him. Bill's first response was, 'OK, well, I need to make some plans.' Pierre explained he'd been headhunted by a new company. Bill said, 'I'm shocked. I wasn't expecting it.' Silently Pierre wondered how Bill could be shocked since he'd never taken the time to get to know Pierre and probably had no idea what motivated him. It wasn't just with Pierre. Bill had a reputation for his cold and detached leadership style—when he was told by department members about personal matters that might impact work, he was awkward, uncomfortable and dismissive. They simply stopped sharing.

Throughout the time they'd worked together, it wasn't just that Bill was impossible to reach, but that whenever he was physically in the room, he wasn't really present. He would enter into a room unprepared or unfocused, repeat conversations they'd already had, and ask questions that had already been answered, clearly not recalling that they'd moved on from them. Bill sometimes remained texting on the phone whilst meeting with team members—and on an unforgettable occasion he even kept his feet on the table, soles pointing towards Pierre whilst he stood in Bill's office and began conducting a spontaneous performance review of a project. A colleague later shared the reflection that Bill clearly felt at ease with Pierre— Pierre, on the other hand, reflected it felt like disrespect.

Bill probably believed he was a good leader. He ended the conversation with Pierre by saying that he was unhappy with Pierre's decision and that he did value him even though he might not have shown it. Pierre said he'd been given a great opportunity that he couldn't refuse. Because that's what they tell you to say, to not burn bridges. If Bill would have been open to constructive feedback on his style, Pierre might have shared it, asked for an exit interview or confided in a senior, but he knew, however, it was pointless. Bill was entitled.

PEOPLE DON'T LEAVE JOBS, THEY LEAVE LEADERS

Leaders cannot simply expect respectful regard based on their position or title. Everything they say and do happens under the microscope of employees and stakeholders, who may be quick to point out flaws and inconsistencies. Words and actions have more weight and authority than the title, so the challenge is in being more careful, adaptive and filtered whilst still having integrity and authenticity.

Leadership literature is full of strong rhetoric stating that people don't leave their jobs, rather they leave their leaders and the toxic cultures these difficult leaders create. When good people leave without warning, leaders must ask themselves, 'Did I not know? What could I have done differently? What difference would it have made if I'd known earlier? Where are my blind spots?'

When leaders are surprised by their employees' aspirations, it's simply a sign they don't know them—and they're not really doing their job as a leader. Take, for instance, the standard departure letter, which is, 'Dear Leader, I've been given an amazing opportunity I can't possibly ignore. I've had a great time at this job.' Consider what the letter doesn't say. The smart albeit unhappy employee will have given at least some thought to the content and rather than write, 'You've been a great leader, and I can't imagine ever finding somebody like you again,' to a poor leader, they leave blank silences in relation to the leader's skills or their relationship together. The message is in the absence, not the presence of words.

In the case with Bill, there was a clear gap between intention and impact. His shock and dismay at Pierre's news show that he didn't feel his intentions had been well understood. His style of leadership was to let team members get on with their jobs and not get in the way, which at one level is what is needed, particularly at senior leadership levels. But he only had half the equation. Leadership is not about being absent until required. It's about being present and directive and 'seeing' your employees. When employees say they wish the leader was more visible, what they are really saying is that they want to be valued, heard, recognised and understood. Being physically present in itself is of little consequence.

All leaders fall somewhere on the continuum between the fully engaged or fully entitled leader. Where the needle falls on the continuum reveals the beliefs you hold about yourself as a leader. By becoming aware of your beliefs, and confronting and managing them, you're able to move along the continuum towards engaged leader. PIN and

ABC enable you to move the needle, but first, you have to understand your starting point.

EIGHT COMMON DYSFUNCTIONAL BELIEFS OF LEADERS

Leaders don't get the engagement they want or need often as a result of their own beliefs they have about themselves as a leader. We all have blind spots that keep us from being our best selves.

Far too many leaders believe they're doing everything right. They are most often mistakenly confident about their leadership skills, their power and how they are perceived by their teams. A dysfunctional belief is a firmly held belief (that in an extreme form is a delusion) and is usually resistant to change—that belief often creates a mindset that in turn, creates the blind spot. Many people have firmly fixed beliefs about their leadership and are resistant to getting into a learning mode or modifying their beliefs. At the extreme end of the spectrum, they will counter feedback and advice on their difficult leadership style with aggressive defensiveness or point out the proposer's faults in an attempt to shift the blame and pain.

As you read the various types of dysfunctional beliefs held by some leaders, I ask you not only to nod your head when you recognise these in a leader you've had or your own colleagues but also honestly acknowledge the twinge of recognition in your own leadership beliefs. Use the descriptions below to first benchmark where you are on the leadership continuum. No one is a perfect leader and self-awareness is the first step to changing the way you lead.

1. 'I'VE STUDIED LEADERSHIP, SO I'M A GOOD LEADER.'

Some leaders believe that having read a book or two, gone through a leadership program, or attended countless conferences or seminars automatically makes them an effective leader. As one senior leader proudly shared with her team, 'I've been on the best Leadership Program with Professor X.' Sadly, that association had not translated into effective leadership as she suffocated her organisation with stifling micromanagement to become more like her. And yet, just because they can talk about what effective leadership is or cite a few known authors, doesn't mean they know *how* to lead. However much they have 'done' doesn't mean they've trained and put into action the 'learned' strategies or behaviours. Knowledge in and of itself does not make an effective leader.

This principle is true for all of us. Think about trying to change your eating habits. You may have read a lot about healthy eating, you know what's good for you, you may have followed a program or even hired a nutritionist, but have you actually transferred what you know into what you do, or the habits you've formed? Have you restocked your cupboards with different food? Have you stopped buying snacks that you know aren't healthy? When you go to a restaurant, do you resist ordering food that you normally would and make a healthier choice?

As psychologists are quick to point out—and employees with poor leaders will point out, too—having good insight isn't enough to make a behaviour change. Talking the talk about leadership doesn't translate to being consciously motivated to walk the walk in their actual leadership, nor address your style and impact.

Engaged leaders will be concerned to apply and test their new learning and seek feedback along the way from objective sources to ensure they are on track or seek advice or coaching if they feel stuck.

DIG DEEPER: THE IMPACT OF MICROMANAGEMENT

An organisation that gets used to micromanagement or relentless criticism is easily recognised through employees who show learned helplessness. This notion refers to the idea that if you're taught to be dependant on others—in this case being told how to solve things, or how to do your job the leader's way or no way—you learn to become helpless, i.e., learning to rely on others to solve your issues. Quite the opposite of empowerment and people development.

We see people who accept and passively remain in negative situations all the time. Think of a person who remains with an abusive partner, or the employee who tolerates being undervalued despite having the skills necessary for a promotion. The principle of behavioural theory at play here is often *learned helplessness*.

Based on his studies of learned helplessness,[1] Martin Seligman argued that the passivity or unwillingness to act is often accompanied by feelings of chronic failure, sadness and low self-esteem, claiming those feelings are caused by the learned behaviour of inaction. More recently, however, it is argued by critics that this idea is an oversimplification of what occurs in complex illnesses such as clinical depression.

2. 'I'VE GOT THE TITLE, SO I'M A LEADER.'

The entitled leader wields her authority, power and mandate to get what she asks for. When she demands something, she expects it to be delivered—full stop. She's not concerned about asking things in the right way to create understanding, engagement, or to foster collaboration, and is certainly not interested in her employee's motivation, because she's their leader and they work for her. I call that coercion, not leading.

---

1   Martin E. P. Seligman, 'Learned Helplessness,' Departments of Psychiatry and Psychology, University of Pennsylvania, 1972. Accessed online, https://ppc.sas.upenn.edu/sites/default/files/learnedhelplessness.pdf.

Some may call it delegation, but there's a difference between delegating and giving instructions. Delegation invites the employee to take responsibility for the task or to solve the problem. If you're giving instructions, your team likely calls you a micromanager or a control freak behind your back. What they want is to be invited, not told.

As one leader said to me during a coaching session, 'Why do I need to go to all of this effort? They know they need to do the job and they know I need them to do it.'

I empathise with where he's coming from. It can seem quicker to simply tell your team what to do and have them do it. They will probably do it, too. But the task of a leader, as opposed to a dictator, is to think about the impact you want to have and the type of culture you want to invoke. Do you want people to come up with great ideas, be creative, collaborative, happy to be at work and go the extra mile, or do you just want to get through the day and get the job done? Yes, it can be exhausting, but then that is the job.

Engaged leaders create invitations to responsibility. They have a way of inviting or directing others that makes others want to follow them in spite of obligation and show up with their best every time. They empower others and give them the freedom to come in with new ideas or opinions or challenges. They know when to get out of the way.

3. 'MY TEAM DOESN'T CHALLENGE OR DISAGREE WITH ME, SO I MUST BE GETTING IT RIGHT.'

The leader who makes these statements has a team that leaves much unsaid. Neither compliance nor likability are measures of effective leadership.

Fear and mistrust of the leader often underlie teams who don't challenge their leader, or they are superficially pleasant and conflict-avoidant. They are afraid their disagreement will be met with a negative consequence or judgement, and in some cases, punishment or ridicule. In one case I witnessed, the leader met disagreement with, 'Are you the bad cop here?' and in another, 'Are you sure you wanted to ask that question?' and 'I'm not sure that question made much sense.' His comments were perceived as public humiliation, and his team was loath to speak up.

An effective leader of a great team makes room for collegiate engagement and may even encourage constructive disagreement as a way to pressure test the status quo, or to create new ideas and generate solutions. When the team can express a difference of opinion without risk or fear of retaliation, the impact is that relationships remain intact and trust is deepened.

At the other extreme are argumentative, conflict-filled teams. A high-performing team will regroup and move forward after a disagreement, whilst a dysfunctional team will stay stuck and keep looping. In the latter, one by one, people stop sharing or contributing to the conversation in a passive-aggressive dropout, meaning that they may continue to hold differing views that they will share behind your back but stay silent in your company. A common trait in teams where this is present is the 'say yes but do no' members. You will get superficial support for your idea in the meeting, but when it comes to acting on it afterwards, they will resist or avoid or even become barriers or bottlenecks to implementation. The less-subtle trait is when they stop coming to meetings and answering emails. In short, your team will become 'yes' people. They realise there is no gain in sharing, so they start engaging in an over-compliant agreement or active avoidance.

Likewise, the leader who wants to be the team's best friend is confusing leadership with camaraderie. Over-familiarity breeds contempt as the saying goes and means that it can really be difficult to give challenging feedback to a team member who sees you as a friend. One senior leader complained that his leadership team peers were alienating him. He frequently socialised with his employees, believing that was part of good leadership, but his colleagues felt him untrustworthy. More than likely, his team thought he was a fun guy, but his overfamiliarity meant his peers didn't consider him a strong, impartial leader capable of making tough decisions. The leader must maintain enough distance to exert authority when needed and have difficult conversations without compromising integrity.

Engaged leaders have established trusting relationships with others so that there is an accepted permission to challenge constructively, offer differing views, or advise on alternative ways forward. The threshold for debate is low, and creativity and innovation bloom.

4. 'THE LONGER I DO IT, THE BETTER I GET.'

There's a well-supported belief that the longer you are a leader, the better you get. Leaders often quantify their experience in terms of years, as though time itself is a great teacher. This idea is similar to the myth that time is a healer, as though the passage of time is the source of healing. If this were true, neither post-traumatic stress disorder nor vengeful retaliation would exist. Continuing to train on the same errors over time will simply reinforce them.

An engaged leader who's been a leader for five years can be far more effective than an entitled leader who continues to lead for thirty-five years in the same ineffective way as when she started. Time itself is not the healer nor the teacher; it's what you learn from and do with the passage of time that matters. A leader of a small team responded abruptly when invited to undertake leadership coaching by his own leader. He claimed that he had been doing this a long time and needed no advice, wearing his thirty years as a badge of honour. He mistook an offer for new learning for meaning he was in some way incompetent and defended against his need for it. Since no leader is perfect, there is always an opportunity to learn from others even if only to reinforce your strengths and to make explicit what works or to re-invigorate your tool kit with the latest new ideas and skillsets for ever-changing scenarios and diversity of people.

Engaged leaders understand that continuous learning is at the heart of leadership. They recognise they must stay abreast of trends in leadership itself as well as their business, to ensure they are not out of touch with generational changes in expectations to teamwork or cross-cultural collaboration.

5. 'I WAS A GREAT LEADER AT MY LAST JOB; I'LL BE A GREAT LEADER AT THIS ONE.'

Context is critical. Whilst a leader may have been successful in leading in one company or in a specific role, that doesn't necessarily mean she will be equally effective in every role she takes on afterwards. Every context requires something different or new of the leader and their task is to be adaptable to the emerging demands, challenges and opportunities it brings, notwithstanding the ability to manage the diversity within the new team and stakeholders which will naturally differ in every job. So, there is no guarantee that a great leader today will be a great leader tomorrow. It is the leader's ability to adjust and respond to those differences in the new role that will evidence whether or not they will be effective. And the key is to stay in the engaged leader mindset in every position she fills.

A leader of a small company came into the role from a large corporation. Armed with a wealth of knowledge and experience from the large corporation, he began his daily speeches with 'what I did in company X was' and continued with 'how we did it in company X was.' He assumed that the same tools and processes, together with approach in his style were what the new company needed. He found himself rapidly at odds with the culture of the small company in his attempts to impose his way of working on the teams. They had developed a more informal and needs-based approach to work processes than the formal regulatory approach that would be necessary for a large corporation. The failure in his effective leadership stemmed from a lack of understanding of the differences of business context and ability or willingness to adapt and adjust to those differences.

Engaged leaders are context and politically savvy, learning to adapt as they transition to new roles. They are humble to the reality that when they arrive in a new context, they are also new and therefore know less than most other people they meet there. They will seek to update their skills base and request advice and feedback as they learn to navigate the new leadership challenges.

6. 'THEY PROMOTED ME, SO I MUST BE ABLE TO LEAD.'

People often find themselves in positions of leadership because they've delivered results and been 'rewarded' with leadership positions, not necessarily because they have proven leadership skills or the desire to be a leader. Problems arise when the assumption is 'I'm a great expert; therefore, I'm a great leader.' The skill sets may, in fact, have no overlap at all; the technical expert may have no people leadership skills but is a genius in data analysis, for example. There is no proven relationship between your excellence as a subject matter or technical expert and being a great leader.

If you're a new leader, a first-time leader of a new business, or leading an area that is new to you, you may feel like a bit of an imposter at first. You may wonder how you managed to get the job. No doubt, there's always a first time for every leader when you're not sure that you know what you're doing as if you're doing the right things. It's normal to want to gravitate back to your comfort zone and what you know well, which is often your core professional or discipline competence.

For example, it's often the case that a technical person who's become a leader from within the ranks and now leads a technical department will feel uncomfortable about some aspect of leading and unsure of what to do. In an attempt to regain a sense of competence or feel they can contribute to the team, they'll get their hands dirty by getting actively involved in technical conversations and tasks, albeit uninvited or through thinly veiled attempts at 'guidance' or 'hand-holding,' as I heard one entitled CEO say of his executive team as he railroaded their discussions and red-penned their proposals. In this case, the team may experience the style as micromanagement or interference. The problem lies in not recognising that he's no longer a technical advisor, but the leader. Unless invited, these contributions will be tolerated at best and resented at worst as undermining their competence. It's important for you to learn to accept your new role as a leader is in the empowerment of others to find the best ways forward and to acknowledge that you may not have all the answers despite the competence you came with.

Engaged leaders recognise their limitations when they are an expert in another area yet new to leadership. They know that leadership itself is a discipline that has to be learned and trained in the same way they learned their profession. Acquiring knowledge and regular practise are their best assets.

DIG DEEPER: ENTITLED TO THE EXTREME

This book doesn't address the extreme cases where the needle simply may not move towards engaged leadership. I've heard many a time in the workplace people referring to their leaders as psychopaths or narcissists. Let's be clear for a moment, these are the extreme of the entitled leader. Employees will often feel manipulated and describe the leader as self-serving, egocentric, arrogant, aloof, negative and problem-oriented.

If we want to be specific, we can look to expert and criminal psychologist Robert D. Hare, who created the widely known parameters of a psychopath, most recently under the 'Hare Psychopathy Checklist-Revised'.[2] Symptoms of psychopathy manifest as a general lack of conscience and empathy, as well as a disregard for the law and the emotions of others. Psychopaths often prey on victims through deceit, pathological lying and violence to get what they want.

In 2006, Hare, with industrial psychologist Paul Babiak, wrote *Snakes in Suits: When Psychopaths Go to Work*.[3] Characteristics of

---

2   R. D. Hare, 'Hare Psychopathy Checklist-Revised (2nd Edition) (PCL-R),' In B. Cutler (Ed.), *Encyclopedia of psychology and law*. Thousand Oaks, CA: Sage Publications, 2008.

3   Paul Babiak, PhD, Robert D. Hare, PhD, *Snakes in Suits, Revised Edition: Understanding and Surviving the Psychopaths in Your Office*, HarperBusiness; Revised August 2013.

manipulators in business settings are described as shifting to meet stereotypical gender expectations: a female psychopath might make full use of the passive, warm, nurturing and dependent sex-role stereotype in order to get what she wants out of others and a male psychopath might use a macho image, intimidation and aggression to achieve satisfaction of his desires. The authors posit that around 1 per cent of senior positions in business are psychopaths, but then offer this:

'Nonetheless, based on many anecdotal reports and on our own observations, it is likely that psychopathic individuals make up much more than 1 per cent of business managers and executives.'[4]

7. 'I'M A SPONTANEOUS LEADER.'

Often leaders say, 'I'm much better when I'm not prepared. I just walk in and take it on the fly. I'm a spontaneous kind of leader.' There's really no such thing as overpreparing (unless it gets to the point of increasing anxiety), although it's quite easy to prepare poorly. Let's distinguish between them: overpreparing suggests too much of it, but poor preparation, no matter how much time is spent, is still poor preparation.

Let's take a look at the perception of spontaneity. When a magician pulls a rabbit out of a hat, it looks sponta-

---

4   Paul Babiak, PhD, Robert Hare, PhD, *Snakes in Suits, Revised Edition: Understanding and Surviving the Psychopaths in Your Office*, HarperBusiness; Revised August 2013.

neous—it's magic—but the illusion of being able to take things on the fly comes from a very solid foundation of knowledge that's been acquired and solid preparation that's already been done.

For some leaders, their mental preparation may be invisible to those around them. Others will walk through a full role-play and openly practise what they plan to say. The greatest apparently spontaneous leaders are so familiar with their area of competence or expertise or are so well-rehearsed, they can now do it on the fly. At a certain point in their rehearsed experience, they don't need to spend three hours preparing for a presentation because they've done it many times before and it comes easily.

Spontaneity shouldn't be confused with impulsiveness. Good spontaneity is well-prepared spontaneity whilst impulsiveness is not being prepared. The impulsive leader won't be prepared to address the other's interest and needs, and her lack of preparation shows she's thinking only of her own agenda—more a sign of an entitled than an engaged leader.

Take the leader who decided it was a good idea to have regular town hall meetings. The goal was to inform the whole company what was happening in the business and to invite employees to ask questions, share ideas, give feedback and generally have the opportunity to engage with him. He would prepare his notes well in advance and then use them as memory notes in the room. His intent was to speak in a relaxed, off-the-cuff, friendly, buddy style. His lack of preparation about what mattered to the audience meant that when questions came, he was unprepared for them. He impulsively went off-piste in sharing information that was neither reliable nor aligned with key stakeholders and indeed not wholly correct. On the spot, he made statements and promises he couldn't reliably keep. His impulsiveness led to confusion, anxiety and loss of confidence that he knew what was going on or that he would deliver on promises made in the room there and then.

Engaged leaders know that great performance comes from being well prepared and rehearsed and leaves little to chance. They will be concerned about the audience's needs and be sure to meet them where they are. They understand their role is to create followership and develop others beyond themselves.

8. 'I'M A MAN/WOMAN, SO I AM A BETTER LEADER.'

Last but not least is the dysfunction of a specific bias in who can lead. This can take many forms but the most common perhaps is gender. No doubt some women make far better leaders than some men, but the opposite is also true. I've had my experience of both, and it has been their approach rather than gender that made them stand out. Objective measurement of competence in leadership should drive the choice of leader, though what makes for 'competence' may be itself, a hirer bias that needs addressing. At least, I've yet to see any empirical evidence that simply one gender makes a person a better leader. The Pew Research Center reports in their 'Women and Leadership 2018' survey that 'Few think one gender has a better leadership approach than the other, even though majority sees a difference in styles.'[5] Leaders who still hold onto gender biases may be viewed as out of date and out of touch.

Whilst it is beyond the scope of this book to explore the basis for why there are fewer women in leadership positions than men and the span of factors that relate to that—there is clearly a dysfunctional bias in some people that men make better leaders than women. Take the director I met of a large industrial organisation who, following an enquiry into a major incident, was criticised for his handling of the post-incident review. He quickly defended himself, blaming having women on his team. He believed that women could not lead in a crisis. His dysfunctional belief was that had he had a male-based leadership team, he would have delivered better results.

---

5   Juliana Menasce Horowitz, Ruth Igielnik, Kim Parker, 'Views on leadership traits and competencies and how they intersect with gender', Accessed online, September 2018. https://www.pewsocialtrends.org/2018/09/20/2-views-on-leadership-traits-and-competencies-and-how-they-intersect-with-gender/.

Of course, bias can go both ways; many people believe the world would be a better place if more women were in power.

Engaged leaders value and manage diversity well, and understand that it comes in many forms, including experience, culture, age, gender, expertise, qualifications, attitude and personality. They are nonjudgmental, unbiased and inclusive.

PIN AND EMOTIONAL INTELLIGENCE

What separates the entitled from the engaged leader is emotional intelligence. The basis of PIN lies in emotional intelligence. For the engaged leader, relationships are win-win situations. The engaged leader learns the interests of the team members or stakeholders and is able to communicate the relevance of a task both in terms of the individual's motivation or gain in supporting the task or appeals to their aspiration whilst linking to common business priorities.

The 'sell-in' of a task to a team member or positioning of a request to a stakeholder has to be both authentic and meet the true gains for both parties. Any superficial attempt to simply hang the request onto something the other party is interested in will be experienced as clumsy or manipulative.

Getting this delicate balance right requires emotional intelligence, a term created by researchers Peter Salovey and John Mayer and popularised by Daniel Goleman in his 1995 book of the same name.[6] The definition of EI has two parts: The ability to recognise, understand and manage our own emotions, and the ability to recognise, understand and influence the emotions of others.

Emotional intelligence in a leader is vitally important but knowing what it is only goes so far. What differentiates the engaged leader from the rest is the ability to demonstrate emotional intelligence in everyday leadership behaviour.

EMPATHY IS THE ANTIDOTE TO DYSFUNCTION

All leaders have their blind spots, but empathy distinguishes the effective leader from the truly dysfunctional one. It's about being considerate or kind when there's a tough job to be done or bad news to deliver. It's about guiding and facilitating, not doing. Empathy allows you to demonstrate that you understand what an employee needs and is going through.

The skill here is empathy, not sympathy. Sympathy is about joining and sharing in the joy, sorrow or pain.

---

6   Daniel Goleman, 'Emotional Intelligence,' Danielgoleman.info. Accessed online, November 2019. http://www.danielgoleman.info/topics/emotional-intelligence/.

Empathy is the ability to take another's perspective even if you have not had the same experience where you can offer support and guidance to resolve a challenge. Empathy is not giving the other person a hug, but asking, 'How can I help you, and what do you need?'

DIG DEEPER: HOW MUCH IS TOO MUCH

Vulnerability and authenticity are not the same things. Being vulnerable is part of being authentic, but there is a whole spectrum of vulnerability: relevant vulnerability versus burdening vulnerability. Relevant vulnerability is displayed when the leader shows that she's made (context-relevant) mistakes and learned from them. Burdening vulnerability happens when the leader, for example, tells the team, 'I can't cope.' Leaving the team to pick up the pieces or wondering how they'll manage on her behalf.

On the other hand, when a leader is authentic and vulnerable, their behaviour conveys trustworthiness, which leads to better employee engagement and performance. From a neurological stance, when an employee aligns with a leader, the parts of the brain associated with positivity and social connection light up.[7]

Demonstrating relevant vulnerability is about the significance and context of what the leader shares. If something tragic happens

---

7   Emma Seppälä, 'What Bosses Gain by Being Vulnerable', Harvard Business Review, December 11, 2014. https://hbr.org/2014/12/what-bosses-gain-by-being-vulnerable.

during the workday, putting on a strong face and not telling anybody is not showing vulnerability at all—leaders are human. However, sitting with the entire team and crying is probably not helpful either. Relevant vulnerability is the ability to demonstrate emotions in a contained way. If it leaves others confused as to what to do or how to help you, then it is probably burdening. Asking for help is OK, though dumping responsibility is not.

If you need to get something off your chest or talk a personal matter through, there are better places to do so than with your own team. The better channels would be your personal coach or advisor, the HR department, your own boss or close peer with whom you have a good relationship.

TO LEAD OR NOT TO LEAD—THAT IS THE QUESTION

The idea of 'being' a leader speaks to the notion that you've arrived, i.e., you are a leader. You have the title, salary and the role, but are you actually leading in every moment? Ask yourself momentarily, 'Am I leading now?'

There may be moments when you as a leader step into directing, setting the agenda, facilitating, enabling, empowering, coaching, being curious and supporting. The worst-case scenario is when you step back from leading and into doing or managing. Hands-on leadership is different from hands-in management. The key differences between managing and leading lie in the focus on tasks and people. Leaders are focused on a long-term perspective, creating a vision, setting direction, acting as change agents, developing people and create influence through building trusting relationships resulting in inspired followers. Managers are focused on relatively shorter-term goals and plans, maintaining the daily business and steady operations, developing relevant systems and processes and achieve results through assigning and following up on tasks.

Leaders should set the direction about where the team is headed, but the team figures out the best way and the best tools to get there. If the leader decides the direction, how to get there and the tools to use, she is a hands-in fixer, not a leader, and is likely not focusing on the right things at the right time in the right way. Some use the term *coaching leadership*. Here, too, hand-holding, telling and advising is not coaching; a good coaching leader doesn't tell the team what to do but directs or facilitates them to finding their way to do it.

Leading in the moment is like being the conductor of an orchestra. Whilst every musician is an expert in playing their instrument, it is neither possible nor necessary for the conductor to know how to play each instrument. The conductor is the only one who doesn't make a sound yet creates the result and harmony through the orchestra.

As a leader, you shine through the results that you produce through others, not in yourself. The leader is never the first violin but enables the team to perform by getting all the roles to function together. Leading in the moment means utilising the positive synergies in a team and letting those be the shining results rather than the leader being the face of those results.

The solution begins when you shift from fixer mode to curious and learning mode. You're curious about what your team or other people need from you in order to do their work more effectively or to support you. If you're curious, you're less likely to get into telling, interfering, doing and fixing. Here, rather than management, you shift into servant leadership, which is operating from the viewpoint of what you need to do to help others do their job properly, rather than doing it for them.

Choosing not to steer in certain moments might also be necessary. You may be able to step back out of an arena where people are managing their tasks and be an observer rather than being directive. Leadership is also knowing when to step in and when to step out; it isn't always about being busy. You are leading when you are both present and active and present and observant.

HOW ENGAGED ARE YOU?

The bigger or more complex the challenges, the greater the demand on you as a leader to be able to persuade and influence your organisation to see and embrace the changes positively. Some leaders are successful, and some are not. Consider these two scenarios:

An oil and gas company decided to change strategic direction, narrowing its business focus and streamlining its efforts, which meant downsizing. Rumours spread that the cost cutting was solely to line the pockets of the executives and shareholders. The CEO countered the rumours and reduced the noise by linking the change to a higher purpose: without sustainable profitability going forward, everyone could lose their jobs. The CEO spoke to the importance of long-term, sustainable employment and remaining competitive. Whilst some people would lose their jobs in the short-term, other positions would become more secure and purposeful, and the future would mean growth for the business and greater opportunities for employees. Such is the nature of running a business.

In another situation, a senior vice president was charged with reducing costs by 30 per cent across the organisation. He asked his management team to identify efficiency solutions, but then took that feedback and incorporated it into a memo in which he critiqued their individual performances and delivered a reorganisation model, essentially changing their roles and responsibilities. That he did this during their Christmas break and sent it by mail during the holidays was a testament to an overall lack of emotional intelligence and leadership common sense. The impact was a contagious fear that rippled through the organisation as his autocratic and bombastic style established a destructive start to a change process.

Do you lead more like the first leader or the second? How do you overcome your blind spots and distorted beliefs to become the leader you were meant to be?

Being a senior leader can be a lonely experience, with few or even no peers who face the same demands and challenges as you. Few people are willing to give honest, open feedback to a leader. Their natural position of authority and power and ability to hire and fire creates a certain level of fear of retaliation if the subordinate provides candid feedback.

Whilst leadership style and behaviour are the areas where most experienced leaders could improve, it's also the area where they receive the least amount of objective feedback—especially those at the top of the career ladder. In the absence of feedback, leaders believe they're doing a great job—as we saw earlier in this chapter.

How do you, in a moment of leadership, translate all your

expertise and knowledge towards positive engagement with your stakeholders or employees?

In a word, PIN—Persuasion, Influence, and Negotiation.

READY FOR YOUR PIN CODE?

Creating trust is at the heart of building a sustainable business. When you leave a meeting, do you know your reputation outside of the room? Do you know what people say or feel about how you engage them? Do they call you back for more, or do you have to chase them every time? How can you have the impact you need that makes them want to do business with you over and again? If the other party is prepared, wouldn't you want to be also? You need to learn your PIN Code.

PIN provides you and your team a framework, which essentially breaks down your leadership effectiveness into its three component parts, so you know exactly where your strengths and development areas lie and can target specifically where you need to make improvements. Wherever you are on the entitled to engaged leadership spectrum, PIN will help you move closer to becoming truly engaged.

CHAPTER 2

* * *

CLOSE THE GAP

We've all had the experience of watching someone from the sidelines and admiring their leadership ability. Their skills may not always be concrete, tangible or observable from the surface. In fact, it is the subtle arts and nuances of what leaders do that makes it look so natural. Some, of course, are natural-born leaders who are great with people. But great persuasion, influence and negotiation can also be learned, and there is opportunity for you to learn the nuance of effective leadership as well. Let's begin by looking at the three elements of PIN.

PERSUADE, INFLUENCE, NEGOTIATE

PIN is the power of using psychology in business in order to have the positive impact and influence you need to motivate your team and peers, and continuously negotiate with managers, stakeholders or adversaries to make real progress. The keys are in careful preparation, skilled questions, conscious body language and tactical handling of the meeting and the room.

Great leaders infuse PIN skills in everything they do to move their organisations forward with the willing participation of their teams, peers, and stakeholders to create the wins they need. Here are my personal favourite definitions of PIN:

- **Persuasion** is the process by which one person achieves their goal to change another person's viewpoint or position on a matter.
- **Influence** is the power or capacity of causing an effect in indirect or intangible ways.[8]
- **Negotiation** is 'back-and-forth communication designed to reach an agreement when you and the other side have some interests that are shared and others that are opposed'.[9]

We frequently see that *persuasion* and *influence* are used interchangeably. For my purposes, I will focus on the term *influence* whilst recognising that persuasion is one aspect of how influence is achieved.

---

8   'influence.' *Merriam-Webster.com*. 2019. Accessed online, November 2019. https://www.merriam-webster.com.

9   Roger Fisher, William Ury, Bruce Patton, *Getting to Yes: Negotiating Agreement Without Giving In*, Penguin Books; Updated, Revised edition, May 2011.

Leaders spend a good part of their time closing the gap between two opposing opinions. In everyday communications, you might want someone to understand your perspective and see your point of view. Persuasion is about closing the gap between you and your position and the other person and his position. You may need to combine persuasion and negotiation to have the influence you want.

An engaged leader is curious in everyday interactions, asking the other party questions to establish their interest. Armed with answers, he can then start to challenge on facts. Persuasion is often about guiding others to identify the gap between what they believe to be true and actual facts or likelihoods. Parents do it with children. For example, when a child says, 'I don't want to jump off the diving board at the swimming pool because I'm afraid I'll hurt myself.' The parent asks what he thinks will happen. 'Well, I think I'm going to bang my chin on the board when I jump off,' the child says. The parent, in turn, explores the facts in the gap, pointing out that by standing at the end of the diving board, banging his chin is nearly physically impossible because it will already be beyond the end of the board. The child is persuaded to change his perspective by drilling down into facts.

Robert Cialdini, an eminent psychologist and author of a

bestseller on the subject of persuasion and influence, is a great read for digging deeper into these areas. Cialdini's point is that humans are persuaded to another person's point of view not by luck but by the manner and methods by which the persuader captures our motivations, interests and what is valuable to us, thereby either motivating us or drawing us in towards the choices they would like us to make.

DIG DEEPER: CIALDINI'S SIX STEPS

In *Influence: The Psychology of Persuasion*, Revised Edition, Cialdini describes those psychological methods.[10] He references six potential paths to persuasion: commitment and consistency, reciprocity, social proof, authority, liking and scarcity.

NEGOTIATION

Negotiation is far more relevant to leadership than you might believe and not just in relation to contract, financial or commercial negotiations where there are rules to follow and margins to maintain. In today's world, negotiations between countries and political parties have huge business negotiations behind them with multiple aspects often related to defence, trade or access.

---

10   Robert B. Cialdini, PhD, *Influence: The Psychology of Persuasion,* Harper Business; Revised edition, December 2006.

Leaders negotiate with other people all the time, and some of the same skills required for effective negotiation are necessary for effective persuasion or influence. The entitled leader may not think he is negotiating or believes he shouldn't have to because people are employed to do the task the leader asks. Negotiating implies there's an option of saying no, which there is, of course, and yet negotiating is about creating the win-win in which the opportunity is framed. Yes, the employee may be obliged by virtue of their role to do the task, but creating a culture of willing collaboration rather than coerced delivery is the difference between an effective negotiating leader and an entitled one.

DIG DEEPER: HARVARD'S SEVEN ELEMENTS OF NEGOTIATION

Harvard's seven elements are interests, legitimacy, relationships, alternatives and BATNA, options, commitments and communication. If you want to know more about this approach to negotiation, there are a number of great sources, including Bruce Patton's contribution to *The Handbook of Dispute Resolution*.[11] And their executive programs offer hands-on education in their approach at Harvard's Program on Negotiation at the Harvard Negotiation Institute.

---

11   Michael L. Moffitt, Robert C. Bordone, editors, *The Handbook of Dispute Resolution*, Jossey-Bass, 2005.

There's an overlap between some of the skills required for effective persuasion, influence and negotiation in these models. Specifically, Cialdini's model and Harvard's model both emphasise reciprocity, interests and relationships.

We see these tactics in operation in our daily lives, but we can use them consciously in business. Drawing on Cialdini and Harvard and the great wealth of literature on what effective influencers do, I suggest that the skills of great PIN leaders essentially fall into these three categories:

Establish trust. They do this easily and focus on what they have in common with others early on. They do it quickly and often through reciprocal exchange of personal interests. The shared information doesn't have to be private, but it is often personal. These leaders are open about themselves and interested in others as well. Their body language (which is discussed in chapter four) and conversational style (chapter five) is inclusive and focused on commonalities.

Diversity is a big buzzword today. Be it gender, sexual or cultural diversity, the idea that different perspectives create greater value is huge rhetoric in business. Differences in opinion bring different ideas to the table. Those who want to harness that diversity, however, to have influence with their team, especially in a direction that might be challenging or unpopular, will start with a focus on a common goal. They emphasise the need to pull together because of the impact the change will have on the group as a whole. Diversity brings the data whilst influence makes use of it.

Demonstrate empathy. They use empathy, not sympathy, to try to understand the other's perspective. It is the ability to put yourself as a leader in someone else's shoes to both establish their motivation and interests or see their point of view that builds trust and allows you to explore together opportunities for influence and mutual benefit. You expect doctors, for example, to have empathy; they don't need to have a broken leg to understand that you're in pain and need a certain treatment course. Psychologists empathise all the time. They may not have had the same losses or traumas as their clients, but they know enough about how the loss affects people that they can empathise and help patients find a positive way forward. Influential people demonstrate empathy through active listening (which I'll explore in-depth in chapter five), mirroring the words of the speaker.

Remain curious. Under pressure, pushback, resistance or conflict, they stay in curious mode, searching for information to help them understand the other person's perspective. They use this data to then offer a different perspective based on evidence and facts, if helpful, or indeed that curiosity may lead to a shared understanding and agreement that was not obvious at the start. Simply put, they seek data to elicit whether their assumptions and opinions are correct. Great influencers are able to neutralise assumptions by drilling down for facts and staying curious.

When two parties are exchanging information, both need to be equally open (reciprocity) to build trust. In both cases, you need to understand the other's motivation and interest, which is all about building relationships.

BUILDING TRUST

The basis of willing and winning relationships is trust. What would you do for someone you trust as opposed to someone you either didn't know or actually mistrusted? For example, if you're a complete stranger to a co-worker whose help you need, and you don't have a formal mandate, then you must present your case to get onto their priority list amongst the million other things they need to do and justify why your needs should secure a place on their agenda.

In organisations, trust is universally recognised as the foundation upon which high-performing teams are built. Without trust as the foundation and glue between members of the team, the ability to reach their full potential is severely limited. Take military teams as an example; the need to trust each other literally with each other's lives is at the core of their ability to pull together and perform under extreme conditions.

FUNCTIONS AND DYSFUNCTIONS OF A TEAM

In the business context, I look to Patrick Lencioni, who developed his Five Dysfunctions of a Team model for explaining the hierarchy of pitfalls teams face in working together. Absence of trust is the biggest cause of dysfunctional teams, followed by fear of conflict, lack of commitment, avoidance of accountability and inattention to results. Whilst there are hundreds if not thousands of models that describe what teams need to do to function well and deliver results, I like the simplicity and clarity of Lencioni's model, which I find leaders easily understand and relate to in daily work:

In *The Five Dysfunctions of a Team*, Lencioni uses the pyramid below to explain the causes of dysfunctional teams.[12]

---

12   Patrick Lencioni, *The Five Dysfunctions of a Team*, Jossey-Bass, 2002.

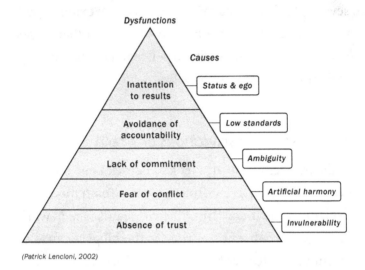

(Patrick Lencioni, 2002)

Lencioni defines the Five Functions of a Team as follows:

1. Trust is the foundation of a functional team. When team members trust each other enough to be vulnerable and open with each other about weaknesses, fears and behaviours, they set themselves up for success in the next four levels.

2. Teams that trust each other are able to engage in productive, constructive disagreement and conflict that leads to the team's or organisation's ability to exploit their full potential.

3. Teams that resolve challenges and conflict make better quality decisions and then commit to those decisions they make because the team has clarity and alignment.

4. Committed teams hold each other accountable to high standards.

5. The apex of the pyramid, supported by the four prior levels, is achieving collective results, where the health and success of the team overrides individual egos and silo-based agendas.

Lencioni's Five Dysfunctions of a Team are the polar opposites of the functions. Team members don't trust each other, they fear conflict and they are unwilling to commit to decisions or be accountable, all of which leads to poor results.

THE FIVE FUNCTIONS OF A TEAM

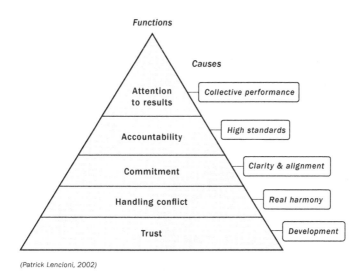

(Patrick Lencioni, 2002)

The question I often get from leaders is 'I know that trust

is important in teams, but how do I actually build that in practical terms?' I have sought to answer that in this book in a simple step-by-step approach built on both well-published psychological research and my experience as a clinical psychologist.

In 1977, a psychologist named Bruce Tuckman described the five stages of development within teams: forming, storming, norming, performing and adjourning.

DIG DEEPER: TEAM DEVELOPMENT

For more information on Tuckman's original model: forming, storming, norming and performing, see his article describing the first four stages: 'Developmental sequence in small groups'.[13]

In a revised article, he added the fifth stage, adjourning. Complete information can be found in 'Stages of Small-Group Development Revisited'.[14]

The stages start from the time that a group first meets until their purpose ends. Psychotherapists in clinical settings with patients have described the same processes in building relations, whether in groups or between individuals. In my approach here, I have adapted these to

---

13 Bruce W. Tuckman, 'Developmental Sequence in Small Groups', *Psychological Bulletin*, Vol. 63, 384-399.

14 Bruce W. Tuckman, Mary Ann C. Jensen, 'Stages of Small-Group Development Revisited'. *Group & Organization Studies*, 2(4), 419-427, December 1977. Copyright © 1977 by International Authors, B.V.

propose a simplified model of how trust is built between individual people from when they first meet each other, perhaps at a networking event or when new in a job or team, to how that relationship develops over time building trust along the way.

STAGES OF TRUST BUILDING

(Adapted from Tuckman 1965)

Two parties move from one level of trust to the next as more personal information is exchanged and the relationship grows.

Trust building begins even at the first meeting when two people don't know each other very well, if at all. At this stage, superficial common ground is established and the conversation circles around commonalities such as working in the same company, knowing someone in common or living in the same neighbourhood. The conversation is sprinkled with questions such as, 'Oh, so you know Mario Rossi.' or 'Have you been to this conference before?' or 'I really enjoy that TV series, too.' This is safe ground for both parties, and a thin layer of trust is established based on a pleasant interaction and mutuality. For a new leader meeting the team for the first time, this conversation focuses on saying hello and shaking hands, maintaining a light touch in mutually sharing where they have been, their common experiences, backgrounds, networks and social interests. If they decide they have nothing or very little in common, they will not move to stage two and stay at the superficial level of engagement at stage one.

When two people establish what they have in common and like each other, they are more willing to go deeper when they meet the next time and then more open to listening to each other.

When the two parties meet again after the stage one encounter, they move to stage two. Stage two lasts longer and the conversations run deeper, moving beyond common ground questions and answers into more personal and values-based sharing. Questions here venture into a more personal level and tone and may sound like, 'You said you have two children. How did you spend the weekend? I prioritise family time, too, and I spend as much time as I can with my children above work.' The conversation still seeks common ground but touches on what motivates and drives both people and what they value. Over repeated encounters, more and more is shared. We remember the stories and can pick up on those each time we meet, thereby giving a feeling of knowing each other.

When solid common ground is established at the second stage, trust has reached a strong point. Both people feel they have more in common and see the world in more or less the same way. They value people, time and resources in a similar way. They begin to feel connected and because they know each other better, they are willing to deepen and build on the trust they have.

Whilst it sounds like a simple phase, it lasts several encounters and builds like a steep slope rather than the pillar shown in the diagram.

Stage three begins when you've met repeatedly, and common ground has been established. The two people have now perhaps been colleagues for a significant amount of time. They've spent social as well as work time together and exchanged quite a bit of personal information. The relationship is on much safer, solid territory, and can tackle those conversations on which long-term relationships are built. In stage three, one person can ask for support from the other. If there's a conflict, productive dialogue ensues without risking the relationship. Because they have enough trust to move on from common ground, they may discover differences related to politics or religion, but the established relationship is strong enough to respect those differences.

The differences or disagreements don't threaten the foundation of the relationship, because it's standing on a good deal of trust and solid ground.

At stage four, the relationship is able to manage and indeed benefit from differences of opinion and differences of ideas and perspectives. They can utilise disagreement, even where it might be a conflict, for testing out and shifting their own perspectives, gain new insights and continue to deepen the trust through mutual sharing and learning.

Understanding how we build trust sheds light on why conflict may occur when two people first meet. Without the trust that comes from first establishing common ground, there's no motivation to accept another's difference of opinion or decision. For example, if a new leader comes into a team and immediately gets into conflict conversations with team members over opposing priorities, for example, and without getting to know the team or letting the team get to know him, not only might arguments ensue but the relationship is potentially soured beyond saving because those initial judgments are difficult to overcome. They have started at stage three without the solid ground built in earlier stages—they are on thin ice and conflict defines the relationship from the outset.

A leader who can only describe the team members or

colleagues by virtue of their tasks and responsibilities doesn't know them beyond stage one. Should a disagreement or conflict arise, the relationship doesn't have the solid ground of trust to tolerate the differences. Some leaders struggle with knowing their team or colleagues. The engaged leader is curious. He asks questions to find out more than the tasks they enjoy doing. He wants to learn what gets them out of bed in the morning, what motivates them and what they value. It takes time, but it pays off in solid, long-term, trusting relationships.

AUTHENTICITY IN PIN

Regardless of how long you've been a leader or how successful you are, at some point, you're met with challenges where you might struggle to get the support or the buy-in for something you need. You may be presenting a business or investment case, and you're looking for other resources or financial support to be able to continue, and on an everyday basis, leaders are negotiating with employees in getting tasks done, meeting deadlines and trying to get them to agree to the direction they need to go in.

Authenticity, in my view, comprises three elements: consistency, reliability and predictability. Engaged leaders treat everyone with the same respect and empathy, and they do what they say they will do. What's more, they are trustworthy, have integrity and can be depended upon to follow through with their obligations. Lastly, they display levelheadedness as well as steady behaviour and emotions in their reactions to people and situations.

As leaders climb the ladder of authority and mandate, the entitled leaders assume title and power alone will lead to them getting what they need when they need it. They either neglect to see the reality of competing priorities that exist in any organisation or simply feel entitled to getting their share of necessary resources and support in spite of the impact on others. The engaged leader understands that negotiating lies at the heart of getting things done through and with others whilst maintaining positive relationships. This is a fine balancing act where management teams juggle demands for support, resources and finance all the time.

Where the balance becomes even trickier is when, as a leader, you don't have a direct mandate toward the team you lead as is the case in project leadership or functional leadership often seen in matrix organisations or with volunteers in charitable or community organisations. Line management or leadership has different demands than in project management or leadership, which is where you often deal with people who report to other leaders in the organisation. They've been assigned to you as a resource for this project, but they don't report directly to you, so you're steering without real or direct authority. How do you obtain the resources and support without just using your authority and mandate?

If you can't simply mandate someone to do what you need them to do, you have to influence and persuade them in such a way that they will go the extra mile to support your agenda. You will be negotiating with their leaders for the employees' time and prioritisation on tasks for your project. You will need to create the persuasive argument that makes them want to support your needs and priorities.

Don't make assumptions based on bias or superficial data when creating your persuasive arguments and negotiations. In essence, you must appeal to your stakeholders to get agreement to be able to deliver your project with the full scope and resources.

Let's take a look at the most common influence errors.

- Competitive not truly collaborative: focusing on one's own gains at the cost of or in spite of other's needs
- Reactive not proactive: unprepared or taking things on the fly or reacting emotionally without rationality
- Quick to action without pre-alignment: jumping into getting things done or starting to make changes without ensuring key stakeholders or team members are with you and are committed

- Impulsive: unpredictable and unplanned in actions towards others and responses to situations are changeable
- Company-centric rather than having an outside-in perspective: narrow focus on inputs and inspirations for driving change or innovating
- Hierarchy rather than information-driven: tendency to assume that people with the titles hold the information you need rather than looking for actual information or insight bearers
- Know-it-all attitude as opposed to a learning attitude: not open to others' points of view or new information. Often resistant to advice from others, even experts.
- 'If it's not broken don't fix it', approach: rigid or inflexible approach to the way things are done around here and closed to improvements or efficiency measures where it may mean changing the status quo

Authenticity in persuasive argumentation is essential. Otherwise, like a bad salesperson, a thinly veiled attempt at hooking into your motivation can be at best off-putting, and at worst feels coercive. Take this example: A managing director and investor, David, wanting Jane, a senior colleague, to invest in his new start-up company, began by saying that he knew she had a daughter with a long-term illness and that family values were important to her, so the best thing she could do was to think of how this company investment would give the long-term financial security she would want for her daughter. Whilst his intentions may have been in the right place, his reference was a clumsy attempt to find a link and perhaps even emotionally exploitative, to appeal to Jane's values and create alignment with the offer. He came across as inauthentic, however, and he missed an opportunity to establish Jane's actual interest in this investment and ran with his misjudged assumptions instead.

DIG DEEPER: FIGHT OR FLIGHT

When you're exploring and trying out these strategies, you may wonder whether there's a real science to all of this or whether it's all based on some notional theory or simply pop psychology driven by self-help ideologists. Well, there's actually a real neuroscience to what we do, the impact our actions have on others, and whether or not others respond to us in a positive way. For example, you may be familiar with the 'fight or flight' response to anxiety or stress, a term coined by Walter Cannon in 1915.[15]

If you're on the sidewalk and see a bus veering off the road towards you, you will run away and not try to stand and take on the bus. Likewise, if a person is physically threatening to harm you, you may decide to run away because you don't have the strength to

---

15 Walter B. Cannon, 'Bodily changes in pain, hunger, fear and rage: An account of recent researches into the function of emotional excitement', New York, NY, US: D Appleton & Company, 1915. https://doi.org/10.1037/10013-000.

overpower them or you may choose to fight them. In business encounters, the same reaction takes place. When someone behaves aggressively or tries to coerce you and you feel a threat to your opinions, beliefs or values, the same part of the brain is triggered. If you feel cornered or bullied by someone, you may become defensive and fight back, or you may decide to leave.

Likewise, living creatures, including humans, have a physiological response to rewards or praise.

There is enormous literature and easy to understand descriptions on the internet about how people respond to threats or rewards. We should be mindful of how powerful our influence can be. There is a neuroscience behind effective influence, and in its simplest form, we see the physiological reaction that poor tactics, such as aggression, coercion or bullying trigger compared to best tactics, such as rewards or validation will trigger.

Let's take a simple look at the scientific basis for influence tactics and their effects. On the one hand, we see that poor tactics may trigger part of the brain that feels under attack or threat (associated with serotonin), creating a flight or fight response and a desire to avoid that experience again, resulting not in willing collaboration, but coercion, and thereby achieving only short-term results. On the other, we see that the best tactics may trigger part of the brain that responds to reward (associated with endorphins), creating a more cooperative response and desire to repeat that positive experience, leading to a willingness to collaborate, and thereby achieving longer-term results.

So, getting it right is about authentic impact. The other party willingly wants to join you in your endeavour and likely wants to follow you over time to collaborate on winning together.

THE IMPORTANCE OF EMOTIONAL INTELLIGENCE (EI OR EQ)

It's not uncommon that the EI (or EQ as it is sometimes referred to) skills I am purporting, which are the focus of many HR training programs for leaders, are referred to as 'soft skills'. The use of this term somehow infers that they are easy or nice to have and on the side of so-called 'hard skills', which are deemed necessary business-related skills that are often technical or core discipline knowledge-based. By such categorisation, soft skills development and training often become the victims of budgetary cuts when times are tough. Who wouldn't cut spending on nice-to-haves when the business is struggling?

Yet, I have to challenge this notion of soft skills and the inference of their dispensability. If leadership were not about leading people, but operating machines, then naturally, focusing on how to motivate the machine, encourage a machine to collaborate with others and resolve differences or agree which machine should produce first or ask for help from the other machine when new ideas are needed, etc. would be unnecessary. You get my point. It is impossible—yes, impossible—to conduct a successful business that is dependant on people doing the work without focusing on how those people are motivated to do their job. Positive motivation will get you greater, more sustainable results than 'motivating' through fear or coercion.

Leadership is about the people who are doing your business. We have leaders because of the human element of getting things done; if you decide not to focus on the human element, you will be the factor that limits the potential. Leaders must ensure they know how to bring out the best not just in individuals but also in teams to deliver results that impact the bottom line.

DIG DEEPER: BUSINESS CASE FOR EMOTIONAL INTELLIGENCE

Thankfully, many a smart and successful company has seen the benefit of investing in EI skills development in their leaders and teams. For a thorough review of research read the 2016 report 'The Business Case for Emotional Intelligence' by Joshua Freedman and

Paul Stillman of Six Seconds (The Emotional intelligence Network). The evidence has shown that emotional intelligence is more than twice as predictive of business performance than purely cognitive intelligence and is more predictive of business performance than are employee skills, knowledge and expertise.[16]

In their report, the findings are startling. EI training at Fortune 100 companies showed significant financial gain after senior leaders were trained and followed up in EI. Freedman and Stillman write, 'For example, at PepsiCo, executives selected for EQ competencies generated 10 per cent more productivity, 87 per cent decrease in executive turnover ($4m), $3.75m added economic value with over 1,000 per cent return on investment. High EQ salespeople at L'Oreal brought in $2.5 million more in sales. An EQ initiative at Sheraton helped increase market share by 24 per cent, whilst Amadori experienced a 63 per cent reduction in turnover and manager EQ correlated positively with plant performance'.[17]

Leaders often struggle the most with influence in lateral relationships. Because a direct mandate doesn't exist, leaders may tend to neglect the very relationships that are crucial to everyday leadership and getting the work done.

---

16 Gerald Mount, 'The role of emotional intelligence in developing international business capability: EI provides traction'. In V. Druskat, F. Sala & G. Mount (Eds.), *Linking Emotional Intelligence and Performance at Work* (pp. 97-124). Mahwah, N.J.: Lawrence Erlbaum Associates, 2006.

17 Joshua Freedman, Paul Stillman, 'The Business Case for Emotional Intelligence', Six Seconds (The Emotional Intelligence Network), December 2016. https://www.6seconds.org/case/business-case-ebook/.

In working across silos—whether cultural, geographic, or organisational—emotional intelligence plays a key role in building the relationship you might need further down the line.

You know your role and responsibilities, your priorities and what the business does. You know you're supposed to lead, inspire and motivate your team and encourage collaboration. You know all the *whats*. Your PIN Code is *how* you take what you know about your business and your mandate and get to that point where you are truly inspiring others and fostering the culture your business needs. PIN is the conduit, the connector and the bridge between your head and what you know and the reason for being in the role and responsibility.

It's called leading in the moment—it may look spontaneous, but there are practises to apply in every moment. Practises that may feel uncomfortable and awkward at first but as you apply them consistently, they'll become part of your mindset and way of leading, until you, too, are the leader that others admire from the sidelines.

The next chapter presents the A of ABC—the approach and advanced preparation required to persuade, influence and negotiate with others. The chapters that follow address B for behaviour and C for conversation.

CHAPTER 3

***

A IS FOR APPROACH AND ADVANCED PREPARATION

The memo Sandeep wrote piqued the executive team's interest. He was invited to pitch a business case for an organisation-wide project on introducing a new way of training safety personnel. Early in the conversation, however, Emily, the CEO, jumped ahead, asking for details about the benefits the project would provide and why so much money should be invested in new technology development. Emily's agenda reached wider than the one Sandeep was addressing. She wanted to know the long-term impact the project would have on the future of her company.

Sandeep asked Emily to indulge him for a few minutes whilst he walked through his proposed plan, and then painted a picture of it. Sandeep asked Emily to imagine employees in various countries in operational environments accessing updated training requirements on an app on their phones as those requirements were revised. The project would enable employees all over the company on the same installations to receive feedback and updated training in real time wherever they were.

Now Emily understood the importance of investing on an improved IT structure. They budgeted, talked about alignment and taking out waste, and improving strategic focus and privatisation. But in the moment, she wanted to see how it worked on the ground day to day. To those in the room, it may have looked like Sandeep could think quickly on his feet and had responded spontaneously. The truth is, he had prepared that scenario beforehand, and researched Emily's interests and learning styles and knew the type of questions she might ask. Without preparation, Sandeep would have lost the engagement.

GROUNDWORK: APPROACH AND ADVANCED PREPARATION

This challenge of translating your agenda and ideas to others comes up for a lot of leaders who are in receipt of a new strategy, goals or initiatives that they need to communicate to an organisation. You must believe in and fully understand the agenda yourself in order to motivate and inspire others whether those dependant on you for that direction or the decision-makers for supporting your cause. By knowing your audience, you're able to involve them to see what you see.

What typically gets in the way of leaders' communication? What are their typical strengths and blind spots? We all have lenses affecting our assumptions and feelings, and these may stem from some or all of the following:

- Our culture and personal values
- Our home organisation and its role or perspective
- Our individual personality traits

So, how do we avoid falling into the blind spot trap? The most important starting point is with them—not with you. You need to firstly:

- Consider their values and interests. Think through why they should listen to you.
- Link to business strategy or their priorities, so they see what's in it for them. Show you care beyond your own area and title, so they don't feel your request is entirely selfish for personal gain or glory.
- Don't assume or judge what they will offer or may resist. Be curious: where can you learn the most? Who

can help you understand your counterparts and their drivers and needs?

- Be prepared for and invite the right stakeholders to meetings or conversations, so you have the possibility there and then to get a commitment to the matter on the table, thereby avoiding having to refer to it elsewhere or cause delays.

Remember: You don't know what you don't know, so investigate and research beyond your own sphere of insight.

Let's take a deeper look at the two sides of approach: the mindset you bring and the research you do.

DIG IN: A LEADERSHIP MINDSET

The biggest and most common leadership mistake is the idea that 'It's all about me and my agenda that you're here to serve.' It may come at the cost of a collaborative mindset and be indicative of a competitive one, such as 'In order for me to be successful, I have to gain something to win, and so you have to give up something to help me get my job done. I am your leader after all.'

A well-known exercise I learned at Harvard's negotiation program demonstrates the tendency for people to go into competitive rather than collaborative mindsets whilst co-working with others. Even with the best will in the world, we often tend to take in what we need rather than listen to what is being said.

In this simple exercise, participants engage in a brief activity, which is akin to arm-wrestling though it is not described as a wrestle, more so that it is the posture two people will adopt for the purpose. The instructions are simple: both people have one minute to move arms to and fro, and a point is awarded each time your arm brings the other's down onto the table, and your personal goal is to get as many points as possible. The points gained by the other person do not affect your score.

When the clock starts, invariably people start to 'wrestle' trying to resist the attempts of the other person to score points. The mindset being competitive, 'I have to get as many points as possible, which means for me to win, you must have to lose.' Even though it's not called a wrestling match, people assume they should wrestle. People begin to forcibly try to beat the other person, so they get more points whilst the other person gets fewer.

Nowhere in the instructions does it say that you have to get your points at the expense of the other person, or that you have to get more points than they do. Having undertaken this exercise numerous times, some pairs will get a one-zero score or zero-zero because they've battled each other into remission, and both lost. Some people who understand the task have reached scores of 111-111!

The key to success here lies in a pre-game strategy conversation: having actually understood the task is about both parties getting their best personal high scores, winning teams agree up front to jointly move their arms in unison to and fro as fast as possible, thereby giving both the same high score. The collaboration win-win is in action.

This one-minute exercise often surprises people because they believe they're great at collaboration, but then they go straight to the biggest mistake most leaders make.

BIASES AND FILTERS

We all see the world through our own biases and filters, often without knowing it. Bias comes in many forms. It may be towards gender, culture or some professional groups, such as tax collectors or parking attendants, or simply towards people we don't like or connect with. On the other hand, some may have a bias towards supporting the so-called underdog, like welfare organisations. Knowing your biases is part of your mindset.

A filter, on the other hand, is looking at only a part of the situation. If you always apply the filter of potential risk and failure, you may miss out on seeing opportunities and benefits. If you always apply the filter of cost saving, then you may miss the opportunity for a good investment.

Psychometric tests can help you identify your blind spots, or you can ask your peers and team for feedback. It's important to know which biases and filters help or hinder you as a leader, but that is not the end game in itself. You must know what to do with that insight. How do you make sure your filters don't create missed opportunities or correct them so that you don't make erroneous assumptions or draw incorrect conclusions?

It's a challenge that is of particular concern in companies where taking risks, thinking out of the box or where creativity in new ideas, solutions or innovation is critical to their growth and survival against the competition. Let's take a tech company dependant on new product development to beat the competition. At some point, the team tasked with coming up with new ideas prepares to present their case to a senior management team for sifting and selection of best opportunities. Typically, the process is that the ideas are filtered through a funnel of various viability criteria, including cost, speed in getting them to market and relevancy. When you get to the end of the funnel, out pops the most viable product or idea.

I have seen many a management team shoot themselves in the foot by becoming the very barriers to new ways of thinking that they are trying to encourage...and cannot see it. Is it about a mindset that is 'risk confident'? That in itself, no doubt, causes concern for leaders in any sector where technical development and safety go hand in hand, for example, manufacturing, construction or oil and gas. Yet, they also hinder and compete with one another. Safety concerns by their nature are risk averse and organisations with a core safety dependency can have a tendency to 'say yes and do no' when it comes to support-ing the innovation agenda. Experience shows that even the best intentions can fall foul to the final safety card in management decision-making. Project teams with radical new ideas face inevitable challenges as cautious decision-makers apply their filters and lenses of gloom relating to a range of barriers from 'Can we really afford it?' or 'What will the authorities, regulators, stakeholders or even colleagues say?' to 'We can't take risks.' Even the best of minds and talents creating the greatest of ideas may find themselves subjected to the boardroom 'funnel of gloom' as I call it. Think of it as the dark side of capital value processes. It's not about favouring risks to lives or material assets, but an attitude that is open to creating options without the filters as a mental straitjacket. The filters, which may have been appropriate at one time, may not even be relevant anymore but the company ends up with stagnated ideas as a result.

GREAT NEW IDEA!!!

AUTHORITIES
REGULATIONS PROCEDURES POLICIES
BUDGET LIMITATIONS PROCESSES
RISK AVERSION OUT OF TOUCH LEADERS
OWNERS HISTORY
CHANGE FEAR
STAKEHOLDERS

SAME OLD IDEA?!

PREPARE YOUR MINDSET

Many tools involve preparing for a conversation or meeting by conducting analysis, acquiring data and learning about the people you will meet. The importance of mindset for a meeting, on the other hand, is emphasised far less.

Advanced preparation isn't limited to researching the other person and practising your speech. The mindset you carry into a meeting will leave its mark on everyone in attendance. If you're irritated because the previous meeting went poorly, everyone in that meeting will shift into a poorer frame of mind. The consequences go beyond the meeting at hand. Your mindset may be as indelible as a tattoo, and the next time you meet with the same group, they might put up their walls and barriers, because they don't want to let you create a bad atmosphere again.

Your mindset is tangible. Let's be honest, we all have met people we don't like at work but nevertheless have to work alongside or collaborate with at any point in time. Without being conscious of it, your feelings towards that person during an encounter may be visible to them. You might as you approach them already be thinking, 'Oh no, I don't really want to have to ask for her help but I'm going to have to' and by the time you get to speak to that person you are feeling irritated and defensive. That mindset will be visible on your face and body language if you are not conscious of addressing it.

If you keep the following in mind as you enter a meeting, it will show on your face:

- Approach it as a game of win-win, not a battle, and find common ground.
- Adopt a positive attitude. If you are not feeling good about the other person or situation, doing the opposite behaviour helps. Put a big smile on your face, unlock your arms and stride with confidence towards the meeting, intentionally believing that this is a new opportunity for the encounter to go well. The effect on your demeanour will be far more subtle than you fear, and you are unlikely to come across as smiling manically but more that it will counter the frown you would otherwise have arrived with.
- If you anticipate resistance, appeal to their wanted quality. What is it they want to be perceived as? Could

you appeal, for example, to their desire to show flexibility, generosity, compassion or supportive nature?

- Be aware of your own blind spots and biases and check them at the door. Remove assumptions about the other person and how they might react. Stay open-minded and curious—you don't know the future until you get there. See it as an investigation of a new opportunity.
- Empathise with their interests. What drives, concerns, motivates or occupies them now? What might be in it for them to listen to you or support your needs?

Whether you're in a positive frame of mind or you feel worried and concerned, that's going to show in your facial expressions, broader body language, perhaps tone of voice or choice of words. You will need to check your mindset before you begin. If you're going into a meeting to recognise the success of your team, you will want to be positive. If you're worried because you just learned that a peer has been made redundant, take a moment to leave that worry at the door. Doing business is as much about delivering results as it is stopping still and reflecting. Few leaders pause between one meeting and another to ask themselves what mindset they will carry into the next conversation and how that will be perceived by others.

Once you have adjusted your own mindset, you must consider the person or persons on the other side of the table.

By thinking about the other party, successful, engaged leaders distinguish themselves from entitled leaders.

DIG IN: DO YOUR RESEARCH

Leaders often neglect to research the person they are dealing with and rather focus solely on the business context and task. Some may think this is unethical, but on the contrary, if you were going to interview someone, you would look at their social media profile, read their CV and speak to people who might have worked with them, maybe even get feedback from informal references. You do that research to figure out as much as possible to help you cooperate with that person and see if there's a good match between them and the role. Likewise, leaders need to know how someone handles themselves under pressure, collaborates on a team, or what their communication style is like.

You then need to manage the insight you've learned about them. If you've learned through speaking to their peers and counterparts that they don't like your company and they have a particular issue with a colleague of yours, you can prepare to encounter hostility. If the person is your neighbour's sister and she's told them personal information about you, that would be helpful for you to know.

Are you willing to take the time to consider what the

other person needs from you in the conversation? Are you open to adopting a mindset characterised by being willing, inclusive and inviting? You have a task; perhaps you must deliver a workshop with high expectations or invite others to a discussion about how to reach a challenging goal. You understand the journey, but how do you get there?

Psychologists often use the phrase 'finding the hook in the other person'. In speaking with clients, they ask questions to understand what motivates the client or appeals to them to make the changes the client desires, then use their tools to help them. In this way, they create a connection. They also begin to build trust along the lines of the trust model. You look for the hook that makes a person want to willingly cooperate.

DILIGENT PLANNING

Whilst it may be obvious in many cases that preparation is important ahead of meetings, presentations or negotiations, there is an art to planning.

What do you need to know and for what purpose?

First impressions count and influence counts longer, so be prepared to give more than just a good impression. Leave a footprint, so to speak. You want to leave an impact that makes them want to seek further connection with you or at least talk well of you or recommend you to others if this was a one-off encounter. This means knowing the other party as well as possible.

Research and establish their interests. This may take some very careful research, for example, searching on social media, speaking to co-workers, colleagues, neighbours, common friends, previous employers, etc. Find out what drives this person, and what they are interested in when it comes to supporting you in your endeavour and what priorities they have that you can link to. Depending on your context, i.e., addressing a difficult conversation or potential conflict, you might need to know what triggers them or irritates them in order to be prepared for emotional reactions or pushback on your ideas.

Use networking opportunities to build trusting relationships (as explained earlier in the Trust Model) and authentic rapport. This is a skill often overlooked, and many leaders dislike it perhaps because it can be seen as a purely instrumental or transactional focus to relationship building, i.e., we are talking because we might need each other. It can be uncomfortable if leaders find small talk difficult or struggle with initiating conversations with strangers. Prepare some icebreaker questions ahead of the meeting or event or have two or three that you can always pull out of the bag if caught off guard. The internet is full of tips on this subject. The rule of thumb is to get out of your own head and the worry of how you will be viewed, but instead to be curious about the other party and what they are about.

Prepare a simple list of questions starting with where you are. For example, if you're at a conference event, ask, 'What brings you to this XX event?' or 'What has stood out for you today? What did you think of the program or X speaker?' If meeting in other contexts such as cocktail events, you might start with, 'What's keeping you busy these days?' or reference something in the news that is neutral or relevant and be prepared to offer your view on it or ask, 'How was your weekend/summer/winter?' The other person may also find networking uncomfortable, so try to see it as an opportunity to build knowledge about each other in a light way and mutually curious way.

If starting a new job or task, stakeholder-mapping is your best friend. Know your stakeholders:

- Build alliances long before you need them. You never know when they might be helpful further down the line. Don't only link to people you need now.
- Think about whether you are influencing the right person in the right way at the right time? Know your purpose or objective in choosing this person.
- What power, authority or mandate do they have?

Build relationships with key influencers rather than the nearest target or people with impressive titles.

- What interests and triggers them? Start where they are, not where you wish them to be, i.e., what's important for them right now, or how are they feeling about the stage of the project, process, or deal at this time?

In a project where you are working out who your key stakeholders are and their interests, consider using a tool called RACI. The acronym stands for Responsible, Accountable, Consulted and Informed. Use that as a way to identify the people involved in each task or at each stage of the process. In this way, you limit over involving people who aren't necessary to the task and also avoid excluding people who need to be informed.

Map who you need to know now and later. Then build a relationship with them. If you don't have access to the person you need to influence, e.g., the decision-maker, then find out who influences the decision-makers—and it's not always obvious who that is. It could be a friend, neighbour, work-related advisor, or personal assistant. Find out and start there.

- Once you do that, ask for their help, support or advice.
- Ask what they need and hook your objective onto it.
- Understand their personal situation, so you can be

sensitive to it or refer to it when you next meet to deepen trust, and learn their story, so next time you meet you can follow up on it and show interest.

- Know their organisation, needs, drivers, and priorities.
- Plan to leave your desired impact.

In almost all cultures, reciprocity and consistency are key to building relationships. Mutual sharing or exchange of information is important—you both need to know each other—it doesn't work if it's a one-way street. Being reliable and consistent are highly valued. People like to know where they have each other and that lies at the heart of trusting relationships. What does a trust-based reciprocal relationship look like? It can be based on the stages of the Trust Model:

- **Shared interests:** Personal, work, family, leisure, hobbies, friends (Stage 1)
- **Shared values:** Work, personal, family, spiritual, aspirations, hopes, drivers (Stage 2)
- **Shared goals:** Tasks, projects, assignments, to achieve success, to do a job well, to feel competent, to deliver quality, to have a good day at work (Stage 3)

THE ROLE OF FANTASY AND VISUALISATION IN PREPARATIONS

I have long been interested in how successful individuals plan, strategise and execute and whether there was indeed a biological basis to it or whether it could be learned. We all know people who are disorganised or always late to meetings, and we also know those who seem to always be prepared and on time. Perhaps we see these differences also in their performance—some people seem to always deliver great presentations, speeches, or results and others seem clumsier, ad hoc or unpredictably successful. In my work as a forensic psychologist, I took this interest into the perhaps more extreme area of studying the difference between offenders who were seemingly predatory (very organised and planned in their offences) compared with those who were more opportunistic (disorganised or unplanned). I wanted to know what differentiated them. To my fascination, the literature led me to the role of fantasy or creative visualisation in planning and successful implementation in those offenders who organised their crimes and planned far ahead in the execution of them. We've heard of organised crime—bank robbers, drug barons and terrorists are all well-known to have preplanned their activities in detail well in advance to elude apprehension and secure successful implementation of their intentions. In my research, I looked at those who carefully planned their offences and those who were seemingly more impulsive and opportunity takers.

DIG DEEPER: FANTASY

In my specific research[18] into the role of criminal fantasy in predatory and opportunistic sex offending, I was interested as to what degree fantasy provided an internal forum for preparation and rehearsal of later criminal activity. The idea is that the individual is likely to engage in a series of progressively more accurate trial runs in an attempt to enact the fantasy as it is imagined. They mitigate risks along the way by adapting the intended plan as new information comes to light through behavioural tryouts. In the case of a criminal, the goal of the fantasy is to ultimately elude apprehension. So, the bank robber might imagine or visualise the approach to the bank in stages. For example, first to assess the location and ease of access before imagining how to overcome the employees and security. In the early stages of imagining this, he may decide to try out accessing the bank as a normal customer on a particular day to see how many security guards are present and where the security cameras are, or the access to cashiers. This information is then later added to the visualisation or fantasy, which then helps rehearse the next phase in planning. The fantasy snowballs in detail as it grows, giving an elaborate and more exacting picture and the plan gets clearer. Naturally in the area of criminal fantasy and sex offending, the trial runs may present themselves as escalating in seriousness of sexual behaviour from more minor non-contact activities such as voyeurism to more serious and extreme behaviours resulting in contact with others such as rape and murder.

---

18   Nashater Deu. 'Executive function and criminal fantasy in the premeditation of criminal behaviour'. CBMH (Journal of Criminal Behaviour and Mental Health) Volume 8, Issue S1, November 1998 Pages 41-50. Copyright © 1998 Whurr Publishers Ltd.

My learning was that the more elaborate the fantasy used to pre-plan, imagine and rehearse intentions, the great likelihood of that plan being executed successfully.

There have been numerous attempts to define and explain the experience of fantasy and although there is no general consensus, there does appear to be considerable overlap between definitions of fantasy, daydreaming and imagery. Functional explanations have characterised fantasy as a learned thought process that allows individuals to create a type of mental picture. This picture comprises a group of symbols unified into a script in which the subject has a definite role to play in a sequence of events. The script is, to some extent, organised and is capable of dramatisation. What we do know is that they serve as an escape, as an outlet for emotion or a means of regulating one's life.

Fantasy in everyday planning follows a similar sequence. You start with a desire, a goal or a vision of what you would eventually like to achieve, and you may even go on to create the movie, so to speak, of how you would like it to play out. Athletes, for example, use visualisation of winning or achieving their training or competition goals as powerful motivators for their performance.

In leadership, you might think about specific work activities and you play out scenarios in your mind, for example, when preparing for an interview or challenging meeting. You don't call it fantasy, because you associate fantasy with social or personal pleasurable outcomes. But fantasy is merely the thought and visual process of preparation or rehearsal. You have a visual goal of what your achievement should look like and you might imagine what it will take to get there.

When you're planning a presentation, you might visualise or play out the scenario by imagining the answers to these questions: What do you need to know about the size and type of audience? What happens if they ask challenging questions? How do you anticipate the questions they will ask? What if the technical equipment fails? Perhaps you emailed your presentation to yourself and put it on a memory stick. What if there's no technical opportunity at all? You decide to have a flip chart in the room, in case you have to draw it or take a paper copy as the ultimate backup.

Advanced planners have the ability to think strategically about the end goal or big picture and to work backwards and identify the roadmap to the execution of the goal. Using fantasy and visual tryouts that are moderated through an experimental process is a key element to success. Take the speaker. They may walk around the office whilst rehearsing their speech aloud, imagining where they will stand on the stage and looking at the audience, practising tone of voice and emphasis. They might then visit the venue before the big day and walk the actual stage to get a feel for the eventual performance. Considerations such as 'Where will I stand?', 'Where is the podium?', 'How big is the room?' and 'Where will I rest my gaze?' all are addressed in imagined and actual behavioural tryouts. The speaker can then visualise a successful presentation with the audience clapping enthusiastically at the final words. The success fantasy is complete. Building confidence through visual and actual rehearsal gives the speaker the edge in delivering a fine performance when it comes.

You've probably played out a weighty conversation in your head before actually having it, or you've more than likely done at least one run-through before giving a presentation. This is the role of rehearsal through fantasy or visualisation. For leaders, fantasy is a conscious, structured process of preparing the conversation ahead of time—determining how to frame it, and giving the other person the opportunity to explain why something didn't go well.

When looking at projects or negotiations, plan and strategize beyond reaching your goal. What potential scenarios could take place? What are the success factors versus failure factors? As in a one-minute leadership approach, make sure there's no gap between what you want to communicate and what you're actually doing. Much of this is anticipation and planning ahead for various scenarios.

Leaders fail at A when they neglect the momentary check and balance of thinking before they speak and preparing before they act. On the fly is rarely a successful strategy unless you've over-rehearsed.

HELPFUL PLANNING TIPS

Planning how you want the encounter to proceed and preparing your own mindset as well as researching the mindset and personality of the person, team or organisation you'll be encountering are the first parts of preparation. You also want to prepare what you specifically want and how you'll react in the negotiation. Following are a few tools from tried-and-tested sources to guide you into planning your approach to that key conversation or meeting.

When you're learning about your audience, look for clues as to how they want to receive the information. Do they use phrases like, 'I see what you mean' or begin drawing on a whiteboard to illustrate a point? If so, they are likely visual learners and will better receive your message if you include a visual aspect, e.g., slides, diagrams or images. If instead they say, 'I hear you' or sit quietly and listen, they are more likely to be influenced by spoken explanations.

Or, do they often speak of a 'gut reaction' or something 'not feeling quite right'? If so, your message may be best received in a more active situation such as a walking meeting or checking their comfort levels with your ideas. Then, in planning your approach, you can deliver your message in the way your audience prefers.

The same type of preparation should be applied to your rhetoric.

RHETORIC

Rhetoric is the ancient art of using language to persuade. If you're speaking to an audience of lawyers, they'll likely be judging your authority and credibility. If it's a values-driven organisation, such as a charity, you'll need to speak to their values and interests. If you use rhetoric well, your audience will easily understand what you're saying, and will more likely be influenced by it. The three points on Aristotle's Rhetorical Triangle relate directly to the three classic appeals you should consider when communicating:

- Ethos: building trust by establishing your credibility and authority
- Pathos: appealing to emotion by connecting with your audience through their values and interests
- Logos: appealing to your audience's intelligence with well-constructed and clearly argued ideas

We'll come back to the specifics of these types of techniques known as NLP (Neurolinguistic Programming) and rhetoric questions in chapter five, but you should have done your research to find out what your audience prefers as part of the preparation for your approach.

BATNA, WATNA, ZOPA

The terms BATNA and WATNA were coined by Roger Fisher and William Ury in their 1981 book entitled *Getting to Yes: Negotiating Without Giving In*. The first two are the acronyms for the Best Alternative To a Negotiated Agreement and Worst Alternative To a Negotiated Agreement. The text also inspired the concept of the Zone of Agreement or Zone of Potential Agreement, echoed by Howard Raiffa a year later in *The Art and Science of Negotiation*, and ultimately becoming the acronym ZOPA.

If you're looking for financial support or investment from a company for a project, you need to work out where you are likely to agree. It could be financial, contractual or in terms of beliefs, values and opinions. Remember that great influencers focus on commonalities and not differences. They test the limits of their commonalities to determine the scope of their agreements. In other words, how far they can go before they disagree.

If you can focus on what you have agreed to and what's

working, then when you get to the bits where you differ or have conflict, you'll start those conversations from a solid footing. If you jump into the zone of disagreement to start with, it's harder to persuade and influence or move into a cooperative dialogue.

All three terms are well-known in the negotiation world, not just for commercial negotiations but applicable to resources and support or transactions.

Let's say you're meeting the individual, team or group to come to an agreement on a deal. Chances are both sides are offering and asking for something. Your BATNA and WATNA set benchmarks or boundaries that prepare you to counteroffer if you don't like the offer on the table and clearly indicate when to walk away. BATNA and WATNA save you from accepting just anything that's offered, compromising more than you would really like to or giving away unnecessary value.

For example, if you're negotiating a job that offers $50,000, but you could work for your friend and earn $70,000 with all else being equal in both jobs, then your BATNA is working for your friend unless the job matches the $70,000 salary.

Having thought through your BATNA keeps the tone of the conversation balanced. If you don't have a better alternative or have pre-agreed your walk-away point, you may feel taken advantage of and irritated in agreeing to the conditions they set. Whether or not you share the alternative you have, having one gives you a position of power—you don't have to take the deal on the table, and you can negotiate based on confidence that you are not desperate for it. Having a BATNA may be equally valuable to business casing, negotiating resources or investment for your project. If what is being offered is not as good as the alternative you have, then you may decide to either try to get more out of the offer or walk away.

However, let's say you don't have a BATNA and the offer of help on the table is the only offer you have and it's unsatisfactory. Then you are left with rejecting it and leaving with nothing or accepting the best possible arrangement you can. You might, if you are a smart negotiator, manage to integrate additional value items into the unsatisfactory deal like use of office space, access to networks, or invitations to events that increase the value of the deal to you, but costs the other party relatively little. The win-win is sealed.

In the same way, the WATNA is a worse alternative to a negotiated agreement. Let's say you have asked for additional resources to support your project. You may not have a BATNA (no one has the capacity to support you in your team), and your WATNA is having to do it all yourself. In this case, your WATNA will be the benchmark that helps you decide whether you will take what is offered or not—a few resources being better than doing it all yourself.

In the same way that you establish your own BATNA and WATNA, you should also research their BATNA and WATNA, so you're prepared to respond. For example, if you're the one making the offer, what is the better alternative or worst alternative from their point of view? Are they likely to see your offer as better than the options or alternatives they have, e.g. in contracting suppliers, is it better to have you as a customer than not regardless of price?

ANCHORING

Whichever party drops the offer or negotiable number first is anchoring. Most often, dropping the anchor first sets the expectation. For instance, if an employer begins by saying they can offer a salary of $50,000, the candidate's view of the frames for a counteroffer will be affected by the anchor. Even if the candidate was aiming for $75,000 before they came into the room, after hearing $50,000, he might only ask for $55,000, feeling his goal was now too ambitious.

Anchoring is a cognitive bias that describes the common

human tendency to rely too heavily on the first piece of information offered (the 'anchor') when making decisions. During decision-making, anchoring occurs when individuals use an initial piece of information to make subsequent judgments. Not only does anchoring set the expectation, it may also subtly give an advantage to the person who drops anchor first.

Generally, it's important for the leader to drop the anchor first, so his expectations are clear. In communicating expectations for a task, setting direction or a benchmark, think about whether you should be dropping the anchor first and plan accordingly. Is it important to set the expectation or are you curious what the other party wants?

CO-BRAINSTORMING

Co-brainstorming is a process that can be used in dialogues where there is polarised or entrenched opinion or positions and neither party seems willing to offer a different solution or see the other side's perspective. When two parties struggle to agree to terms and conditions on a project or contract and present multiple problems, a co-brainstorming approach may capture everything both parties have said they want, even if they contradict, that both are then invited to critique. The joint brainstorm document can be brought out during the meeting, so both parties can go through it and decide what works or doesn't work for them. The collaborative brainstorming approach reinforces the intent that an agreement will be achieved; it's only a matter of how to get there.

A corporation with many union workers was downsizing and struggling in dialogues with the union as to which tools to use. The union, obviously, wasn't pleased the corporation was letting people go but, because of changes in the marketplace, the corporation had no choice. There were strong, polarised views on what kind of settlements to use to compensate people when they were let go. The meetings quickly became a battle of power and position. Principles started to kick in, yet, if cutbacks weren't made, no one would have jobs at all.

A proposal was drawn up, showing what the broadest possible toolbox for offering settlements and the associated compensation frames could look like. The corporation went through the proposal with the union and asked what things they would keep and what they didn't like. As they went through and negotiated different points, they were clearly already aligning, and the task was how to get there fairly. Through that feedback, the conversation shifted to potential areas of agreement. Both sides had agreed to the big picture; it then became an opportunity to negotiate details.

In a conflict between two employees on a large project

related to timeline planning and resource allocation, the same approach resulted in a shared agreement with trade-offs outlined in both parties' interests.

QUESTIONING

Planning which questions are going to be useful is a key part of preparation. You may get as far as preparing a script that you want to open with. This is what happens in interviews, but the same can be done in leadership conversations. If conducting a performance review with a team member, giving challenging feedback on a task or handling a conflict between yourself and another or mediating between two warring colleagues—think of the kind of questions that will set up a collaborative atmosphere, help the individuals open up and get to the facts and necessary details whilst steering the conversation to stay focused. Anticipate how you will handle strong reactions and emotions or pushback and resistance. Plan what you will say so as not to inflame the situation, or what can you say to ensure commitment to any agreements made. I'll cover specifics of questioning in chapter five on C for Conversations, but planning the questions, conversation and overall steer are key pieces of Approach.

THE VITAL TAKEAWAY

Plan what comes out of your mouth and shows up in your behaviour.

Give it thought ahead of time. Have a respectful consideration of how what you say will affect the other person. Essentially, get out of your own head and into the heads of others.

Leaders often become frustrated that their employees don't understand what the leader means. They often think the employees will just know what a successful delivery is supposed to look like. Why should they know? How has that been communicated to them? How do you avoid the idea that you are setting them up to fail by asking them to mind read?

In your preparation, every context you go into will be different. The context could be that you will have a conversation with an employee about performance, or you may meet with two employees who have a conflict, or perhaps a meeting to pitch a business case and elicit support. Context is important here because when you're planning, you need to research the other party's interests, priorities, needs, challenges, etc., and what drives them. Your planning will be specific to that context.

If you'll be meeting with an employee about their performance on a project that went poorly, spend time determining what the task was, how it was communicated and at what stage it went wrong. If there are three or four people in a room negotiating a contract, discussing the financial aspects can become complex. Research the negotiating styles of those you'll meet with before the meeting. Determine if their patterns are to play hardball or easy and flexible. Learn how important the deal is to them. Plan your approach and strategy for it. If you're going into a meeting with one or more colleagues, then make sure you align your joint approach beforehand.

In Approach, you must be explicit in planning and then expressing your expectations. Don't assume anything, even if it's obvious. State the obvious, just to ascertain that everyone is on the same page.

Understanding the context and the people in it will be key to what you do with the B and C. Imagine walking into a room and you don't know whether you're at a party or business meeting. How will you know whether to be formal or casual in your dress? What are the expectations and the rules of engagement going to be? How formal will this meeting be? You need to do your homework on the situation, people and their interests.

Approach encompasses all aspects of advanced planning: thinking about your PIN goals, researching the needs and personality of the other person or team, identifying your BATNA, WATNA, and ZOPA, practising what you'll say and thinking about potential scenarios and how you'll respond. Remember, what often appears to be spontaneity rests on a foundation of deep and thoughtful preparation. In the next chapter, you'll learn how your behaviour supports your PIN efforts in creating willing engagement.

CHAPTER 4

***

B IS FOR BODY LANGUAGE AND BEHAVIOUR

There are different ways of starting a meeting and approaching a meeting, depending, for example, on the cultural context. Small talk before discussing the business at hand is important in some cultures, whereas in other cultures you get straight into the business and chit-chatting is seen as a waste of time or happens at the end of the meeting. Few behaviours can be as misinterpreted, however, as the handshake.

Something as simple as a handshake can affect the relationship we establish with another person at the outset. We're often more attuned and attentive to our behaviour when the cultures look physically and behaviourally different from ours on the surface. When we engage with a culture seemingly from appearances to be similar to ours, we assume that our customs and behaviours are the same.

When meeting someone for the first time, be conscious and present in those first moments. The foundation of trust begins from that initial contact. It's important to do the homework (Approach) and take the time to be conscious of reflexive behaviour in the moment.

If you make a mistake, name it and bring it into the room. Having the conversation is a learning opportunity, not a failure. Your PIN will be more effective when you learn from those conversations. Showing that you're conscious and aware of the need to try and accommodate the differences and that you're willing to be open, humble and vulnerable goes a long way towards building the trust in a relationship that leads to positive influence.

BEHAVIOUR MATTERS

Social psychology research confirms that first impressions count. Some claim the first three seconds are the most defining seconds of your impact with somebody, and studies conducted by Princeton psychologists Janine Willis and Alexander Todorov show that we form impressions of others in a tenth of a second.[19] All point to the fact that you only have one chance to make a great impression.

But there is a difference between first impressions and influence. I believe that your first impression is so fleeting that it doesn't impact your actual influence. Influence is beyond a momentary impression; it has an effect on the other person so as to create an imprint or change in their position or behaviour built over the course of a relationship, not in a three-, five-, or twenty-second encounter. You won't necessarily influence anybody in those seconds—but you will have made an impact.

Behaviour is important as people often react to what they can see first, then they react to what they learn. What they learn about you, such as your intentions, values or interests, often lie below the surface of your behaviour and aren't immediately obvious.

Humans have a reflexive judgment that causes us to notice behaviour before intention. Unless trained experts, we may make incorrect assumptions based on first impressions more often than right. In the first few seconds of an initial encounter, we use our own experiences and filters, biases and judgments to interpret behaviour. Conscious communication via physical behaviour is,

---

19   Eric Wargo, 'How Many Seconds to a First Impression?,' Psychological Science, July, 2006. https://www.psychologicalscience.org/observer/how-many-seconds-to-a-first-impression.

therefore, important to close the gap between intention and impact.

Let's consider several types of body language as well as the physical environment where your interactions take place and how both can be used to support our messages and procure positive influence.

GROUNDWORK: BODY LANGUAGE

If you're in a situation such as giving feedback or offering support to someone where you need to show empathy and perhaps you've been told that you can come across as a bit cold or distant, then addressing your body language can go a long way in helping you to communicate empathy or sensitivity in a more conscious way. Focus not only on which behaviours will be helpful but also which behaviours might be getting in the way.

Check in and make sure your body language doesn't communicate something you're not feeling. For example, even if you want to be empathic, you may be subconsciously feeling concerned and anxious about whether your advice will be useful or whether the other person appreciates the conversation. Despite your intention to show empathy, your anxieties may be more evident in your behaviour, through folded arms, a furrowed brow or looking down at your lap. You can inadvertently undo the good work, authentic intention and empathy through body language that is getting in the way.

Likewise, you may have a distracting, nervous tic of which you're unaware. Perhaps you click your pen or twirl your hair. How will you find out? Soliciting feedback is important, but the best tip is videotaping yourself in a typical meeting setting and in preparation for a presentation is a good way to identify those habits you don't know about. You will discover things you probably don't know you do and can then address them. Consult with a trusted advisor who can suggest replacement behaviours for nervous habits or distracting mannerisms.

DIG IN

Body language comprises many things, including how we move, sit and stand, as well as facial expressions, eye contact and tone of voice. Let's explore each aspect individually, but remember they work together to create a holistic impression.

OPEN ARMS

People struggle the most with their arms and hands. We may fold and unfold our arms, write whilst someone is talking, hold our phone in our hand and try to glance down discreetly—and these are often subconscious behaviours. (I didn't know I tapped my foot until I saw myself in a video.) Even if you're trying to be conscious of showing you're listening by writing things down, you're possibly communicating that you're not paying attention. It could look to the other person that you're writing your to-do list or are simply distracted by things on your mind rather than listening to them. Does the other person feel heard when you're writing, rather than just looking forward and listening to them?

Folding arms or crossing legs can create a psychological barrier between you and the other person and accompanied with strong words, may strengthen this pose as a defensive or confrontational one. Softer, empathic words may help to reframe the crossed limbs as relaxed. Context is queen in these cases. Generally, crossing limbs abruptly during a dialogue should be given careful evaluation unless the room is particularly cold—it may be that either party is feeling awkward or defensive. You may not mean it to; it may just be a comfortable position. But what if the other person doesn't interpret your stance as comfortable but standoffish? People don't always know you well enough in business settings to know what your normal demeanour is and so are left to interpret what they see there and then. Try to see yourself from the other person's point of view; how might this come across to someone who doesn't know you well? There is an obligation for you to be conscious of what you communicate, so you can bring out the best in each other. Are your actions going to be helpful to the other person? Will they feel that you are really listening to them?

USE YOUR HEAD

Your head often works in conjunction with your hands. Leaning your head on your hand whilst resting your elbow on the table can demonstrate interest. Showing empathy might be conveyed by having the index finger pointing to the temple or ear with the remaining fingers around the chin or mouth. Think of the stance a doctor or counsellor takes whilst listening. The pointing to the ear is a signal effect of 'I'm listening' and fingers near the mouth may indicate 'I'm not talking whilst you are or whilst I'm listening.' The slightly tilted head shows sensitivity and softens the approach.

Don't, however, rest your head in both hands around your face, which may signify boredom, frustration, or intensity that may be off-putting.

EYE CONTACT

Eye contact can be equally difficult for many leaders to manage in showing natural empathy. In a tense moment when someone is complaining or giving tough feedback, maintaining eye contact can feel terribly uncomfortable if not all but impossible. The invisible spider on the ceiling or on the toe of your shoe is suddenly the most interesting point in the room.

Cultural context is key here. Let's take ethnic culture as an example. Indian culture teaches children to remove eye contact when being scolded. Looking down towards your feet and showing the top of the head is a mark of humility and respect for the other. In the English culture, you will more often hear parents say, 'Look at me when I'm talking to you' where eye contact in the same context of being scolded is demanded to show you are paying attention and showing respect for the other. As adults, particularly in business, we need to be thorough in our research to know how eye contact in meetings and difficult conversations may be interpreted—is direct eye contact confrontational or is removing it seen as avoidance, arrogance or aloofness?

Evidence and research[20] show that eye contact prepares the brain to empathise with others. The cerebellum, the area of the brain that's active when we move any part of the body, including the eyes, also contributes to our ability to predict the consequences of actions. As adults, we tend to feel heard or experience empathy when some-

20 Lydia Denworth, 'How Eye Contact Prepares the Brain to Connect', Psychology Today, February, 2019. https://www.psychologytoday.com/us/blog/brain-waves/201902/how-eye-contact-prepares-the-brain-connect.

body looks at us whilst they're speaking and stays quiet in active listening mode and nods to show agreement or understanding.

Even in everyday meetings or encounters where you might know the people you are dealing with, there are still helpful and unhelpful eye contact patterns that should be noted. Some people often break eye contact when they are trying to formulate their thoughts. A short pause is acceptable; anything more can be perceived as rude. Some people even close their eyes to speak. They are likely processing information and need to close their eyes to do that, but it can be off-putting to the other person if you talk to them through closed eyes. Work to consciously maintain steady eye contact without intense staring with the person you're speaking with. Where you stand or sit whilst talking can help with making this feel more natural—we will discuss that later in this chapter.

MIRRORING

Mirroring is an instinctual response that occurs throughout the animal kingdom. In a simplistic way, it happens when one person takes on the same posture or stance as another, creating a mirror image. For example, one person leans into a conversation, and the other does as well or both cross their arms or cock their heads to one side. You can also consciously use mirroring behaviour to communicate your intentions. Mirroring behaviour says, 'We're in this together. I hear you and I value what you're saying.'

DIG DEEPER: MIRROR NEURONS

There's a well-debated theory in neuroscience literature related to the basis for mirroring. Giacomo Rizzolatti at the University of Parma and his team discovered special brain cells, called mirror neurons, in monkeys.[21] These cells appeared to be activated both when one monkey did something and when the monkey saw another doing the same thing. The idea has been linked to humans' ability to show sympathy and empathy. If you'd like to learn more, check out this simple explanation of the theory: 'The mind's mirror: A new type of neuron—called a mirror neuron—could help explain how we learn through mimicry and why we empathise with others.'[22]

If you're communicating effectively, the other person will reciprocate or mirror back. You then get congruity in the behaviour and the dialogue, which can contribute to deepening the relationship.

---

21   Giacomo Rizzolatti, Maddalena Fabbri-Destro, Luigi Cattaneo, 'Mirror neurons and their clinical relevance', Department of Neuroscience, University of Parma, January 2009. https://www.nature.com/articles/ncpneuro0990.

22   Lea Winerman, 'The mind's mirror: A new type of neuron—called a mirror neuron—could help explain how we learn through mimicry and why we empathize with others', American Psychological Association, *Monitor* Staff, Vol 36, No. 9. October 2005. https://www.apa.org/monitor/oct05/mirror.

Overt behaviour is one aspect people react to immediately. When you consciously use mirroring in your behaviour, it has to have integrity. As a leader, when you are true to your intention, and your intentions are positive, then your demeanour will come across as naturally empathic. Often when a doctor is talking to a patient, or a friend listens to another friend in distress, you see mirrored behaviour that comes from true, authentic empathy. People, especially on dates where they are tuning in to each other, have that moment when they discover they both have their heads resting on their hands in the same way, or their legs are crossed the same way. They are mirroring each other's posture without even noticing. It is a strong expression of the subconscious intention.

Being conscious in mirroring is necessary as your behaviour may trigger a reaction in others. For example, if you are angry and behave in an aggressive way, it may be mirrored by the other. They may also react by defending themselves or walking away, but it's possible they will also mirror your anger. Defensive body language can often be mirrored with both parties displaying defensiveness in folded arms, furrowed brows and raised voices, for example.

There's always a cause and effect in behaviour. If you find yourself responding to someone else's aggressive behaviour, you can consciously counter their anger to neutralise the situation. For example, if someone stands up and shouts, you might sit down. People in conflict might say, 'Let's sit down and talk,' which is language that neutralises the possible threat through inviting collaboration.

OPPOSITE BEHAVIOUR

There are times when you have to meet with someone you don't like or has irritating habits. Leaders don't always get to choose their teams and certainly not their stakeholders or peers. You're not likely to be able to persuade yourself to like them in a short space of time, so how do you handle that? One method that psychologists suggest for managing such anxiety is to do the opposite behaviour of what you'd instinctively do. Put a smile on your face, relax your shoulders, let go of the fact that you don't like them, and think about the task at hand.

Opposite behaviour doesn't have to take much preparation, although for a prolonged meeting, a tough negotiation or conflict dialogue, it may need some careful planning and training. But it can be quick—just take a moment to scan your body: is your brow furrowed? Relax your forehead. Are your shoulders up or your arms folded? Let them drop. Do you have a high pitch in your voice? Take a deep breath. Whatever you do when you're tense, what do you need to do to flip that?

Approach comes into play here because your opposite behaviour depends on taking the time to think about what success looks like in the encounter you're about to have, whether it's a meeting or a conversation. It may just be an instant, an image in your mind or something you've written down. But you have an idea of what success looks like, so you know what steps are needed to get there.

FOLLOWING THE DRESS CODE

The way you dress is part of your behaviour or external presentation and is part of your communication. Even in this age of office casual and dress-down Fridays, there are customs and dress codes to follow in different cultures and industries. A financial advisor on Wall Street will dress differently than a Silicon Valley entrepreneur. Spend time to understand the environment and cultural practises to know what's appropriate and that will reduce the noise around you and what you want to communicate or the impact you want to have—so that they focus on your words as opposed to being distracted by your attire. Feel free to stand out and go against the grain—and be prepared for the impact that will have and be even better prepared to handle the effects. There may be times when this is precisely the intention and impact you want. For example, at networking events, where being remembered in a sea of business cards is helpful, wear a bright scarf or jacket that is bold or colourful enough to be remembered for the right reasons.

Clothes can also be an anchor to communicate power or authority and trigger certain behaviours. Take, for example, the use of uniforms in certain professions. From the use of police uniforms to the white coat of doctors to the courtroom judges who might be seen wearing robes, a jabot and a bench wig—they communicate power and knowledge. Some uniforms may trigger certain emotions in others. Seeing a policeman at your front door may trigger anxiety that you have done something wrong or are about to receive bad news. Our mode of dress can be used as a visual cue to create discomfort as well, such as in the legal cases when lawyers suit up. They are communicating that they are not just there to look smart and show they have qualifications, but that they have a mandate and power. It creates discomfort in others that reinforces their authority.

We might use clothing or accessories to deliberately affect our own feelings. Some people have lucky shoes or a lucky jacket, which they wore when they interviewed and got a job. Taking that one step further than luck and associating a feeling of competence or success with something you wear triggers a memory you can draw on to behave in a certain way. Take dressing up for a business style interview—wanting to convey a professional image will affect what you wear—a suit, a jacket, neutral colours, etc. It may lead to you feeling more confident as you walk into the room. In the same way, you can use colour and clothing as a way of triggering or eliciting positive feelings if you are feeling under pressure or stressed in a challenging scenario.

A client of mine, an operations leader, experienced bullying and harassment in a work environment and struggled to attend social networking events. Her experience had left her feeling incompetent and inadequate and was afraid her behaviour would reveal her insecurities. Having discussed coping strategies to boost confidence, she thought about a time when she'd felt confident in the past and remembered her first promotion. She chose the colour purple to represent the feeling of confidence and competence she felt at that time, and purple became her positive feeling anchor. She was to wear something purple to the next networking meeting. She chose an armband, which she wore discreetly, but she used as a memory cue. Whenever she looked at it, she was reminded of the positive experience and feelings she'd had and could draw on them again. She put something purple on her desk next to her computer and started introducing purple when needed as a trigger or anchor point for feeling positive. Psychologists know that thoughts influence our behaviour and vice versa, as is the crux of cognitive behaviour models and therapies. Changing what you think will affect your feelings will, in turn, affect your behaviour. So, recalling a time when you were happy will show up in positive feelings and your body language will convey it. The same pattern is true for negative thoughts.

GROUNDWORK: PHYSICAL ENVIRONMENT

Where you sit or invite others to sit in a meeting is a significant opportunity for setting the stage for the type of influence you wish to have. In a hostile situation that involves a power play such as firing an employee or discussing a lawsuit, you will expect to have different seating arrangements than in a relaxed meeting where the goal is collaboration or support.

In a confrontational or a non-collaborative setting, parties might sit at a boardroom table opposite each other at a 180-degree angle. This setting communicates distance. The table creates a natural barrier, and you'll have very direct eye contact. It will be hard to break eye contact without looking down or away. This seating arrangement is seen in formal scenarios, such as the interview. To promote a collaborative conversation, you probably don't want to sit across from each other, where eye contact will feel intense unless you know each other very well and have already established a great deal of trust.

Sitting right next to each other, side by side is a quite awkward setup. You have to turn your body to make eye contact and the posture can feel strained. The extra effort and unnatural movement make it difficult to remain relaxed and collaborative. Personal space may also be compromised in side-by-side seating. Personal space requirements are different from person to person and culture to culture. Some people require greater personal space, some less. It's simply best not to sit side to side for collaborative dialogue.

Sitting at a 90-degree angle is the most natural and relaxed setup. Whether in a relaxed meeting or in addressing a potentially challenging conversation with an employee—such as a performance review where negative feedback is necessary—you want to build as much cooperation as possible with the other person. Sitting at a ninety-degree angle, or a natural V arrangement allows for side-by-side conversation with easy and relaxed eye contact. Each person is able to hold and release eye contact naturally without having to turn away. This position allows you to sit together and talk something through. It can be done with a table, perhaps with two armchairs and a small coffee table. It communicates a 'we are in this together' feeling with the focus on the task between you rather than each other.

The figure below shows different seating arrangements.

Seating arrangements can reinforce a collaborative or confrontational tone in a meeting.

INTERVIEWS

Some traditional seating arrangements, however, don't psychologically support the people within the context. Consider the setup for an interview.

Often an interview scenario involves seating people directly across the table from a panel of interviewers, a one-to-three ratio or for executive positions even a one-to-five ratio with a big table between you. Everyone will have dressed up, so they are communicating power balance, authority and mandate.

In an interview, however, such a setup doesn't necessarily bring out the best in a person. It elicits direct eye contact, which can often be confrontational. The table between interviewer(s) and candidate becomes a barrier, and with multiple people on one side and one on the other, creating an imbalance of power and authority. It's set up to formalise and further exploit the power imbalance in the room.

The aim of a job interview is to assess someone's suitability for a role, find the best in them, and see if they're a match for the task as well as for the company and its culture. This traditional setup rarely works in terms of making a candidate feel comfortable. We reveal more of ourselves when we're in a comfort zone so that we aren't guarding ourselves. In an interview scenario, interviewers should strive to bring down the candidate's guard, so they reveal more of themselves, rather than encourage them to put their guard up and be sensitised and hypervigilant to every question they're asked.

Of course, there are different set-ups for different purposes in an interview. For example, if the interview includes an assessment of the candidate's performance on a task or presentation of a case study, it may be appropriate to have a boardroom table and projector or flip chart. In the more traditional, dialogue-based question and answer interview, how you sit can make the difference between seeing someone as their natural self (90-degree seating) and an overly worked impression of themselves (180-degree seating), which won't give you what you're looking for anyway. That said, unless recruiters have a good reason for this setup, such as to test an applicant's comfort under pressure and assess their judgment, they should consider using the V or 90-degree angle seating arrangement, or even a round table, for having a conversation.

Nowadays an interviewer will have done their research before a candidate arrives. They will have certainly done an internet and social media search and looked for the person's social footprint. Most candidates would be offended if they turned up to an interview and the interviewer had not learned anything about them, wondering if the interviewer is taking them seriously. It's the same from the other side of the table. If the candidate hasn't done their homework, what does that say about their interest, motivation and commitment to the company with which they're interviewing?

A is important for communicating your commitment to the task at hand and provides the key information and data you will need in the room. B speaks to how the room and seating are set up in the way that will be most helpful. How can you remove the barriers to natural conversation? Then C speaks to the kind of questions you ask. Interview questions are an art and science unto themselves, yet so many interviewers do it without training and are not naturally skilled.

Regardless of which side of the table you're on for an interview, thinking about ABC before the meeting will lead to better results. Maintain eye contact, be conscious of using language fillers, such as 'um', 'so' or 'like', and do what you can to avoid nervous tics such as kicking your foot or clicking your pen.

USE OF ROOM AS CONTEXT

If your meeting must be private, maybe for confidentiality purposes, then, by all means, use a room. If power, authority and mandate are important to communication, choose a room with a table that offers opposite seating.

To hold a relationship-centred conversation, go into a quiet room or even a coffee shop if the conversation doesn't have to be private. As mentioned previously, sit in a V position by taking two armchairs into the room for a relaxed conversation. Think about the impact you want to have and how your physical environment facilitates the conversation.

Sometimes the room isn't necessary. The walk-and-talk is underused by leaders and can be a nice way, especially for people who might find one-on-one facing meetings uncomfortable, to engage in an activity whilst talking that allows for less intense eye contact and more open dialogue—building on more natural interaction. Break away from the need to have traditional, formal settings if the situation doesn't require it. For daily leadership of your team and conversations with colleagues and peers, get together outside of the meeting room and think about what will make everyone comfortable.

DIG DEEPER: MEETING LENGTH

Think about having a thirty- or forty-five-minute meeting with the stakeholders instead of the standard hour, or even having a standing meeting. This immediately signals effective efficiency. Everyone knows to get straight to the key points and focus on those. It's a smarter way of getting to the core issues and taking collaborative action. Ensure, however, that the work that needs to be done in the meeting has sufficient time—don't focus on time over quality.

An article in the *Wall Street Journal* recommends following the Yerkes-Dodson law, which explains how we perform best with some pressure, not so much as to cause stress, but also not completely pressure-free. In meetings, consider how long you really need and then shorten the meeting by a bit. For example, an hour-long meeting becomes a forty-eight-minute meeting. The popular stand-up meeting or huddle has a similar effect in creating efficient, focused meetings. In fact, the article refers to a study that shows sit-down meetings last 35 per cent longer than standing meetings with no gains in effectiveness.[23]

Shorter meetings with deliberate breaks between one and the next like the forty-five-minute meeting instead of the back-to-back hours commonly booked in calendars are also beneficial because you leave time to get technology set up and to get from one place to another. And it gives people a moment to, in a sense, close one part

---

23   Steven G. Rogelberg, 'The Science of Better Meetings', *The Wall Street Journal*, February 15, 2019. https://www.wsj.com/articles/the-science-of-better-meetings-11550246239.

of their brain and open the next, to make a seamless transition free of any stress or baggage you've just acquired in a previous meeting. If you've just had a stressful conversation with someone, you need to vent with a confidante or key party and not take that into your next meeting. Having fifteen minutes between meetings is a good check and balance, to make sure you reset.

STAND UP AND SPEAK

Leaders often speak in front of groups. Common contexts include team meetings, town hall communications or shareholder announcements in a theatre setting, not to mention presenting at professional conferences and giving keynote speeches. Each situation puts the leader's behaviour under the light of scrutiny.

Leaders often forget that a presentation isn't about them conveying information but about how the audience will receive that information. Here, too, their approach, behaviour and conversation support their PIN. Whether in front of a small group in a meeting room or on stage at a conference or town hall, how you stand and move in front of your audience communicates as much if not more than the words you say. It's a frequently purported statistic that what you say only counts for 20 per cent of the effect of your message, whereas how you say it counts for the rest.

Leaders who struggle with public speaking tend to take one of two stances when taking centre stage: cement shoes, where they're rooted to a particular spot and move very little, or pacers, who shuffle papers, walk back and forth or click their pens. Whether they're addressing the team with a simple update or trying to deliver difficult news about a reorganisation, their physical behaviour may distract from the message.

You want to give your message the best chance of being received without distraction, and you want it to be engaging. The speaker with cement shoes lacks personality and is neither distracting nor engaging. The pacer's movements are so distracting, his message is lost. Display authentic feeling and inflexion that go along with your message. You may emphasise key parts of your message by using your hands fluidly without flouncing or taking a few calculated steps without pacing.

Sometimes a speaker in a standing presentation doesn't know what to do with their hands, so they will put one or both hands on their hips. Two hands on the hip can be seen as a power stance. Depending on the context, the speaker may be perceived as confrontational and authoritative because it generates the image of someone about to shout or take over. One hand on the hip can work well when you've got something else in the other hand, like a pointer or the screen clicker.

Unless the presentation takes place in a formal setting such as a keynote address, avoid standing behind a podium. The podium conveys authority and power, think of presidential speeches, and for the most part, everyday leaders don't need them. In fact, the leader who reads from a script behind a podium may be seen a poorly prepared or insecure. A well-prepared, confident leader will be comfortable walking on stage without a podium or prop and use body language to reinforce her message. Even when the podium is required, an experienced and practised presenter will use a three-point head move—glancing right, left, and centre—to make people in the audience feel seen. The inexperienced presenter will stare down at the papers on the podium, leaving the audience looking at the top of his head.

Keep in mind that any noises you make other than speaking will be distracting, so avoid clicking a pen, tapping, slurping on drinks, and shuffling paper. If you must hold something during the presentation, then hold a pencil instead. It still looks like something you'll write with, so people will feel you've got it in your hand for a reason.

When using a PowerPoint presentation, don't stand in front of the screen so half of the image is projected onto your body and face whilst you're talking. Keep animation and zooming to a minimum. Use the laser pointer minimally, because if you're pointing at your presentation, you're not making eye contact with the audience.

As you prepare your presentation, keep in mind the rule of three: people tend to remember things in threes, so place no more than three items on each slide and talk to the text rather than bogging your slide down with details. Limit your final takeaways to three as well. Your audience is unlikely to remember any more than that.

Regardless of the number of people in the audience, imagine you're speaking to one or two people in the room and let your eye fall on those same people over and over. You might feel uncomfortable and think everyone else will feel ignored, but they won't. The fact that you landed on one or two will be interpreted as giving a personal message.

Even if you're going into a presentation with hundreds of people in the room, enter the room before you start to speak, to meet and greet people. Shake hands if appropriate, introduce yourself, and get the name and role of as many people as you can. People will feel, even if you don't look at them in the audience, that you are there to deliver a message to them. The message will be heard differently after you've made that personal connection. The people you met will also be great ambassadors for you and your message when they leave the room.

Being a leader requires skills and confidence in public speaking, and not all leaders have that. The leader who can deliver their message without a script or Power-Point has the most influence with the audience since he can maintain engagement through eye contact and facial expressions to match the message. Your best trick for confidence is preparation and rehearsal. Plan your approach, so you can translate your message in a way that the audience will understand. If you're a bit uncomfortable about standing in front of a group of people and giving a message without props, then overprepare and overrehearse. Say it out loud, not just in your head. That behavioural tryout of how the words will sound coming out of your mouth is key in the practise. You'll be able to practise fluency, rhythm, pace, tone and enunciation, so you sound knowledgeable and secure in your message. Like an actor, you will only deliver well if you know the core message well.

DIG DEEPER: CHANGE MANAGEMENT

In *Leading Change,* John P. Kotter provides perhaps the most practical tool for leaders to look at and prepare for change.[24] It begins with understanding stakeholders and recipients of changes, linking to who you bring into change, identifying the ambassadors and resistors to create the change you need, preparing what you're going to say to people, and lastly, considering how you will manage pushback.

---

24 John P. Kotter, *Leading Change,* Harvard Business Review Press; revised edition 2012.

He recommends preparing the change story carefully and aligning it amongst leadership first, then communicating to the wider organisation—essentially going from A to C. In this case, B would be choosing how to communicate the changes, i.e., via email, in a town hall on video, or in-person in smaller group meetings to allow for questions and answers. I have seen entitled leaders prefer to prerecord messages and send them out, but find this approach tends to be more self-serving. If communication is important enough, engaged leaders should be available for their employees and/or stakeholders.

Dr Elisabeth Kübler-Ross's stages of grief model has been adapted for change management and is now widely used in business for understanding the phases we go through when organisational change happens. In her seminal text: *On Death and Dying*, her model identifies the key stages as shock and denial, anger, and grief (sadness of letting go), which lead to acceptance and moving forward.[25] Understanding where your organisation or employees are in the process of change enables you to better set up your approach to delivering the message and use the empathy required to understand the impact the change has on them.

VIRTUAL LEADERSHIP

Technology today allows us to work almost anywhere in the world. Virtual leadership requires you to consider how to manage relationships through phone calls, email and video.

---

25   Dr Elisabeth Kübler-Ross, *On Death and Dying* New York: MacMillan, 1969.

Again, look at the situation from the other person's point of view; try to understand their context and their world. If you're meeting with an employee, you will need to adjust the room and your behaviour to the expectations of that relationship and context.

Remember the platinum rule: treat others the way they want to be treated, not the way you think you would like to be treated.

If you're meeting with a key stakeholder or customer where you need to convey respectful, collaborative authority, the room and your behaviour should reflect that context and relationship. All customers are not the same, and neither are stakeholders. Think about what they need from the conversation. Do you have to be firm, clear and unmoving from your position, or do you want them to walk away with the feeling they got a good deal out of the conversation and want to do business with you again?

If you're not physically present to explain your expectations and message, you may not have the options of using body language and eye contact. You're left with the options of video, phone call, mail or text. Within that hierarchy, use the one available that gives you the opportunity to replicate most of those skills.

The top of your hierarchy will be video conferencing

because you have nearly as much opportunity to use body language and conversation, the same cues you would use if you were there in person. With high-quality equipment, you can still make good eye contact, use tone of voice and recreate the seating set up.

The second choice would be a phone call where you can still use tone of voice and have a reciprocal conversation. Having several people on a call is always a challenge, so try to limit the number to three. More than three causes too much disruption and speaking over each other. Calls can be great for one-on-one and can be used for challenging conversations if you know each other well, but video conferencing is a better choice with a stranger.

Email and texting are perhaps the worst options for achieving effective influence, particularly in new encounters and building trust. There are many challenges with email: national and organisational cultural differences, writing styles and length, not to mention that words on the page cannot convey intention. There will always be a layer of interpretation to words on the page. Even when you put great effort to get your point across, you are likely to be misunderstood or create an ongoing exchange to get clarification.

In today's world of technology and social media, there should be little reason to rely only on email for big issues and difficult conversations. Video conferencing is pretty much available everywhere now through the use of mobile phones and applications, and face-to-face communication in this way is your best alternative.

Video can work well with good preparation. Video conferencing often has a need for greater efficiency, because you don't do the small talk whilst walking into the room and take time finding your seat. You jump more quickly into the issue you're there to talk about.

PRACTICAL TIPS FOR VIDEO CONFERENCING

- The video setup should be reciprocal so that what they see is what you see. If you only see their head and shoulders, they should only see your head and shoulders (although that's not the best choice). Check that they're not zoomed out and seeing a lot more of you than you thought they were. Don't zoom in to a person's head, so you're talking face to face and nothing else. Try to make it possible to see more of the person's body because then they can use their arms and upper body to add to the communication.
- When video conferencing with more than one person, it's even more critical that you're all seeing the same picture on both sides. Take that minute to introduce yourselves and make sure everyone can see each other on the screens, just basic check-ins to replicate the real physical scenario as closely as possible.

- Try not to sit behind a screen so that you're poking out from behind it.
- Set your technology up ten minutes before you begin the conversation, not when you get into the room. Waiting to the last minute to set up your camera and microphone wastes time and creates a lot of noise. It can interrupt the flow of relationship building and becomes challenging to get the conversation going.
- Avoid eating and drinking during video conferencing. Microphones pick it up, and it's very distracting.
- Turn your mobile phones off in meetings and try not to be constantly writing. Have someone else in the room take notes, so you can pay attention to the screen and people aren't looking at the top of your head.

Show empathy and interest for all parties. If your team is sitting in three different sites and you've ordered a marvellous lunch for your location, be sure to organise for the other sites to have a lovely lunch or dinner as well so that you're all having the same experience. Otherwise, it sets up the idea of an ivory tower that the people in your location have more privileges and probably get more interesting opportunities or greater access to you.

CLOSE THE INTENTION IMPACT GAP

A department management team held a workshop to redefine their HR strategy. During the team's discussion, one team member, Andrew, started to jump in and take over the work rather than listening to what was being said and waiting for the right moment to contribute. Joelle, the team leader, had strong opinions about the topic and was clearly irritated by Andrew's behaviour. Joelle began rocking in her seat, then stood behind her chair until she could no longer contain an outburst. She leapt to the whiteboard, saying she disagreed with Andrew and began drawing and scribbling over what had been written in an attempt to explain what she meant. As she leapt into action, she raised her voice and showed clear frustration with her choice of words. The remaining team members stood back because they could see Joelle was overwhelmed with what she felt she needed to share. They felt sorry for her and her effect was lost in her emotional display.

Both Joelle and Andrew had the intention to contribute, but their behaviour neither demonstrated nor supported that intention. When Andrew leapt from his seat, Joelle, instead of neutralising the situation, mirrored the behaviour by leaping up herself.

Tim, the meeting facilitator, approached Andrew during a break. Andrew was annoyed because he felt Joelle wasn't listening. When asked if he felt his outburst had had the impact he wanted, he said no. Tim suggested that the next time Andrew felt his blood boiling, he remain seated whilst making his point so as to counter the rush of adrenaline that led him to raise his voice and offer unfiltered criticism. Tim had the same dialogue with Joelle.

Back in the room, the conflict of opinion occurred again, but Andrew stayed seated. His voice slowed and softened. He kept one hand under his leg to ground and calm himself. Andrew's delivery was more controlled, and the team saw him as more controlled and considerate. He felt effective and listened to.

In order to close the intention behaviour gap, you want the other person to understand what they hear and see with the combination of your body language and conversation. There must be a good connection between what comes out of your mouth and the signals your behaviour communicates. When there is an alliance between what you say and do, your PIN flourishes.

THE VITAL TAKEAWAY

First impressions count, but influence lasts longer.

Your influence will be most effective when your approach, body language and words are in sync. Be aware of inconsistencies between your body language and your intent or words, because those inconsistencies can mislead your audience and misconstrue the message you want to communicate. Remember that open body language is perceived to be more positive and persuasive, so use your body language, in particular, mirroring, to convey warmth and empathy.

Your emotions impact your PIN code. Stay calm rather than express strong emotions, such as anger or despair, which can lessen your influence and weaken your position. If you know you tend to react to certain people or topics, plan ahead for how you will respond if the situation that triggers you arises.

Decide the arena. First, does the encounter need to take place in a room or would a phone call or email be more effective and efficient? Challenging conversations, however, are almost always better in person in a room. Choose the room size and setup that's appropriate to your meeting and consider whether a meeting is even necessary. Could information be shared ahead of time in an email and the meeting time better used to problem-solve?

How and where the people in the meeting sit sets the tone for the meeting. Set up the room to 'set the stage' for the message you want to share. Consider whether 90- or 180-degree seating will be most effective: 90 degrees being the friendlier, collaborative position and 180 degrees being a more confrontational or power position.

Think about the impact you want to have and choose

the appropriate style for the situation. Do you need to be formal or informal? The clothes you wear and the language you use will be different when you meet with the CEO or board to discuss strategy than when you meet with the department to discuss possible team-building activities.

Consider the tipping points of your audience. Are there points that might lead to resistance or cause irritation? Your behaviour can neutralise or escalate the situation. Thinking about how you'll respond ahead of time goes a long way towards creating a win-win outcome.

As you physically lean into the conversation to demonstrate interest and empathy, listen for confirmation statements such as, 'That's right.' 'I agree with you.' 'As you said,' or 'Exactly.'

In the next chapter, we look at the last piece of ABC: Conversation to align your speaking style, statements and questions with your Approach and Behaviour. You may be surprised that C is for conversation and not communication. All three pieces of ABC support how you communicate your message. C is specific to the questions and conversation styles you use in your communication.

CHAPTER 5

* * *

C IS FOR CONVERSATION

Kathryn, a senior leader, was frustrated and struggling with the executive team's lack of new ideas in a strategy process. In their weekly meetings, few people spoke up or contributed, and outside of the meeting, the team was purely operational, busy with their weekly tasks.

Kathryn had a strong personality. She opened and chaired the meetings and took the minutes as well. She also dominated the conversation, giving her views on agenda items and the key issues. After Kathryn finished her part, which took up most of the allocated time, she would ask the team what they thought. Typically, her question was met with silence, or a couple of people would jump in and agree with her proposal. Because she dominated both the structure and content of the meeting, there was no space for others to speak first and share their competence. Kathryn sought advice. I introduced her to my quick fix tool 'the CEO circle'. This is a technique I have named after I observed its use by effective CEOs with leadership teams where high competence is expected and optimised through empowerment.

In an attempt to change the tenor of the meeting, during each meeting, she delegated the task of taking the minutes and chairing the meeting. Then before speaking, she went systematically around the table and asked each executive for their contribution—everyone had to say something, even if was to say they had nothing more to contribute than that already on the table. Silence was not an option—and the CEO spoke last, primarily filling in gaps, adding to what was discussed or to endorse what had already been said.

The meetings became more efficient, and she saw greater ownership to ideas, involvement and sharing. The team was able to realise more of their potential.

Perhaps PIN comes most into evidence here during meetings. The purpose of a meeting is to create something together and/or reach a collective goal that cannot otherwise be achieved than coming together rather than for the leader to be the only voice in the room above all else. By changing how the meetings were run, the CEO stepped in her leadership role, steering the meeting instead of dominating it.

THE ORCHESTRA CONDUCTOR

In chapter one, an engaged leader is compared to an orchestra conductor. To take the analogy a step further, a leader conducts conversations as a conductor leads an orchestra. The conductor is the only musician who doesn't make a sound. Conversation is not about the leader doing all the talking—in particular, extroverted leaders or those with dominant personalities as in the opening story need to remember this. The leader is responsible for positively exploiting the diversity of perspectives/experience in the room, steering the conversation with appropriate questioning styles and even moments of silence.

GROUNDWORK: C FOLLOWS A AND B

Much of C is a result of planning your approach and choosing appropriate behaviour. There are many methods of steering a conversation to persuade, influence and negotiate with someone. The following is not an exhaustive list but rather presents the methods I believe you might find most useful and easiest to explain in a book.

Your conversations will be most successful if you hone your skills in these five styles of questioning:

- Curious: to resolve conflict, disagreements, polarised ideas, resistance or opposition
- Circular: to dig deeper, for example into values, motivations, drivers
- Confirming: to ensure you've understood what was said, data is correct, showing empathy
- Clarifying: to determine meaning and intention, exploring ideas, rationales
- Challenging/Investigative: to test a situation or hypothesis, provoke opposing or new ideas, open up for pressure-testing existing ideas or concepts.

DIG IN: STEERING THE CONVERSATION

Following are explanations for several types of questioning styles and in which situations they are most effective.

KNIGHT'S MOVE

In the game of chess, a knight's move is two links forward and then one to the side. In clinical psychology, the term describes a style of thinking that is linked to thought patterns associated with some forms of psychosis. If you're speaking to someone with acute psychotic illness, you might be on a conversation track that you expect to go a particular way, such as, 'How was your holiday?' 'It was lovely.' 'What did you enjoy doing?' 'I particularly enjoyed sailing on the lake.' A few minutes later, however, you find yourself talking about whether the sales at this time of year offer great bargains and you can't work out how you got there. The conversation has moved from sails to sales, and you're confused because the conversation is no longer where it was planned to be.

DIG DEEPER: DERAILMENT

We all lose our train of thought or digress sometimes. Some of us have a harder time following a linear structure of conversation than others and go off on tangents, and particularly under pressure or stress, this is quite natural and nothing to be concerned about. In psychiatry, it becomes a thought disorder—called loosening of association or asyndetic thinking—when a patient's impaired capacity to sustain coherent discourse occurs in their written or spoken language.[26] The discourse consists of a sequence of unrelated or remotely related ideas. When spoken, the frame of reference changes from one sentence to the next, leaving the listener, if not both parties, confused.

Knight's move in this business context is neither derailment nor tangential thinking. It's an effort to consciously steer a conversation when Speaker A chooses an aspect of the last statement of Speaker B and moves the conversation to the side. For example:

---

26 American Psychological Association Dictionary of Psychology. https://dictionary.apa.org/loosening-of-associations.

Speaker A: 'What did you enjoy on holiday?'

Speaker B: 'I enjoyed sailing. The water was lovely and warm.'

Speaker A: 'I love being active on holiday—have you ever tried hiking?'

Exploring other preferences loosely related to the main topic helps the sharing to broaden the dialogue beyond the initial topic, and this can lead Speaker A to ask questions about other aspects of the Speaker B's experiences, values and beliefs.

In a leadership meeting context, you might encourage leaders to use knight's move consciously, especially when conversations are stuck. If the team's discussion is becoming too narrow or focused on only one aspect of the issue, or perhaps becoming focused on one solution or problem-orientated, you might consciously throw in a statement or question that is linked to the discussion but brings everyone on the right track. If on the other hand, two people are arguing and becoming caught up in an unconstructive debate, you might use the move to break up the dialogue and shift it into a constructive one.

A curious, engaged leader might use a knight's move question for further investigation into relevant content and to establish people's interests to broaden a discussion for fact-finding or find the motivational hook—all in order to serve the other party's needs whilst meeting their own. It is by learning about the other person that you can use PIN to create willing engagement and win-win situations.

Politicians are masters at using knight's move to avoid questions or speak to their own agenda. A leader can find knight's move to be a useful tactic when he's been cornered with a question that is too prying, for example. In those cases, the knight's move is a way to respond politely and move on rather than create an inappropriate confrontation.

You can also counter a knight's move with a knight's move. Perhaps every time you try to talk about personal development and performance with an employee, he brings up issues with other people, their poor performance or talks about how much work he's been given rather than how he's prioritising his own. You need to keep the conversation on track by talking about prioritising and the resources they need or have. Be conscious of when you're being drawn into a knight's move, so you can bring the conversation back on track.

CONSIDER THE AUDIENCE

Remember the platinum rule: it's not about how you'd

like to deliver the message, but how the receiver would like to hear the message. Your conversations will be more effective if you use language, questioning and conversation styles that resonant with your listener.

We all receive information and learn best in one of three modes: some people are visual learners, some are auditory learners and some are kinesthetic learners. Neurolinguistic Programming, or NLP, relies on these three modes to question and converse with others. The brain makes links between experience, language and behaviour, and this can be used to help us understand other people. The goal isn't to change people, but to understand what their neurolinguistic preference is for receiving and learning information. NLP provides a great framework for understanding the way to frame your feedback or question, so the other person gets what they need.

A visual learner, for example, will tend to draw whilst trying to explain something. They'll use phrases like, 'I see what you mean.' or 'I can picture that.' They understand concepts best when they're written down or illustrated. If you sit and simply talk to a visual learner for an hour, they're likely to get distracted and not retain the information. Show them a diagram or a chart and take them on a visual journey of explanation and ask, 'Can you picture this?'

An auditory person learns best when they hear something, and will use phrases like, 'I hear what you're saying.' or 'It sounds like a good plan.' Receiving through hearing is more important for them. Attempts to visually show your thoughts to an auditory learner may not be perceived the way you intend, and they may even be distracted if they have to look at an image whilst listening to you speak. They need to hear the arguments through active listening, as opposed to written down. An auditory person might prefer podcasts, rather than written articles.

A kinesthetic learner prefers to learn through feelings. These people may be better at taking information whilst they're doing something. It's easier to have a conversation with them whilst they're walking along with you than sitting across the table from them. They use phrases like, 'It doesn't feel right.' or 'It doesn't feel good to me. I'm having trouble understanding that.' Appeal to their feelings and ask, 'Does this feel comfortable to you?' or 'Are you ok with this?'

The point of NLP questions used in this way is that by paying attention to the mode of learning the other person prefers, you can adapt your questioning style and ensure that the message is received by the other party in a way that they prefer to receive it, thereby increasing the likelihood that it will be understood and remembered. This is key to closing the intention-impact gap in conversation.

For example, I wanted to send some information to a client before our next session, and I asked how she would like to receive it. She said not to send anything written because she hates reading long articles. When I asked how she tended to learn, she responded that she listens to podcasts in the car all the time. Instead of the usual articles and PDFs, I sent her a link to some podcasts.

LADDER OF INFERENCE

The Ladder of Inference is a well-known influence and negotiation tool. It was developed by the American Chris Argyris, a former professor at Harvard Business School, in 1970. In 1992, The Ladder of Inference became popular after being described in the bestseller *The Fifth Discipline*, which Argyris wrote in collaboration with the American scientist Peter M. Senge.[27]

People are often led by jumping to conclusions. Sometimes these can be correct, and other times they're wrong, which then later leads to conflicts with other people. The Ladder of Inference uses questions to move from an assumption or myth to reach a fact. It can help you to no longer jump to premature conclusions and to reason on the basis of facts and see the other's perspective. In climbing down your ladder and theirs together, review-

---

27   Peter M. Senge, *The Fifth Discipline: The Art & Practice of the Learning Organization*, Random House Business Books, first edition 1992; revised edition Doubleday, 2006.

ing the available data provides an opportunity to check the validity of the assumptions based on what you can discover and learn about each other.

Leaders often find the Ladder of Inference technique helpful in conflict management. If you have two people who are taking positions and arguing their points, you can use the Ladder of Inference to break down assumptions that are holding them back from getting to the facts.

As shown in the image, the rungs of the ladder correspond to thinking stages during a discussion or negotiation. As more data is gathered at each rung, the involved parties can challenge the facts and draw better conclusions. As you climb up or down from rung to rung, you must ask yourself *what* you are thinking and *based on what information*, so you can compare your reality to the facts and adjust your reasoning, assumptions, or conclusions. Likewise, you can challenge another's reasoning and assumptions with your facts and data.

The Ladder of Inference describes the thinking process that we go through to get from an assumption or conclusion to a fact-based decision or action. The thinking stages can be seen as rungs on a ladder, as seen in the graphic.

LADDER OF INFERENCE
by Chris Argyris and Peter Senge

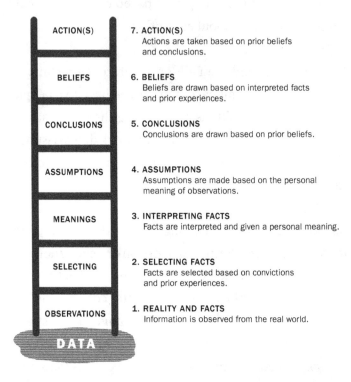

ACTION(S)	**7. ACTION(S)** Actions are taken based on prior beliefs and conclusions.
BELIEFS	**6. BELIEFS** Beliefs are drawn based on interpreted facts and prior experiences.
CONCLUSIONS	**5. CONCLUSIONS** Conclusions are drawn based on prior beliefs.
ASSUMPTIONS	**4. ASSUMPTIONS** Assumptions are made based on the personal meaning of observations.
MEANINGS	**3. INTERPRETING FACTS** Facts are interpreted and given a personal meaning.
SELECTING	**2. SELECTING FACTS** Facts are selected based on convictions and prior experiences.
OBSERVATIONS	**1. REALITY AND FACTS** Information is observed from the real world.

DATA

Our conclusions and beliefs are formed based on our interpretation of the facts, but not necessarily the facts themselves. We take actions that seem right because they are based on what we believe. All too quickly, we jump to conclusions by missing facts and skipping steps in the reasoning process.

With the Ladder of Inference, we can return to the facts and through reasoning, confirm our beliefs are based on the facts rather than a narrow field of judgment.

When two parties disagree or a situation goes awry, the Ladder of Inference offers a way to guide the conversation and come to resolution. At each rung of the ladder, you can ask questions to test and confirm the data set of facts that have been selected, their meaning, and that your assumptions, conclusions, beliefs and actions reflect the facts rather than your interpretation of them. On the way up from the bottom, ask yourself—and the other party—what you think and why:

- What facts are the basis of the discussion?
- Why were those facts selected?
- What meaning have we given to those facts?
- What assumptions may be incorrect?
- What conclusions should be revisited?
- What beliefs should we consider changing?
- Where might our actions be wrong?

Along the way, you may need to adjust your assumption or broaden the data source that provides the facts.

The Ladder of Inference works in both directions. If you've already reached a point of taking an action that's being questioned, ask the questions in reverse order:

- Why did I choose this action?
- What belief led to it?
- Are the conclusions that led to that belief sound?

- Are the assumptions valid? Is the selected data appropriate?
- And are there other facts to consider?

It's easy to subconsciously skip a rung; go through each deliberately and affirm the answer before moving to the next.

We are all on top of our ladders at some point, and when we disagree on something we feel strongly about, such as politics or religious views, we take a position. If the other person's conclusion is different than ours, we'll each continue in those positions, battling over which one is right and which one is wrong.

On the ladder of inference, you start at the top and ask yourselves questions to determine the data on which you are each basing your conclusions. Maybe you've judged someone as aggressive and hostile because you have only ever met them in that one challenging context, in a business meeting, and that is your only experience of them. Maybe you think they are just being difficult in not supporting your idea, but the facts show that they were actually concerned with security or risk of the new plans. You realise that there's a whole pool of other data about each other and you can access that by going down the ladder. With this new information, you gain new understanding of each other, and you may well end up changing your original, erroneous assumption.

When something goes wrong, people tend to ask why. Think of the parent who is upset with a child and asks him, 'Why did you do that? Why did you break it?' The blaming or accusatory tone of why creates a defensive reaction. If a project manager, for example, turns up in the leader's office to give the news that the project is drastically over budget and will miss the delivery deadline, the leader often questions why that happened. The 'why' becomes something that drives a personal accusation and a shift in accountability and responsibility solely to the employee.

Asking 'Why' is great for understanding root cause analysis, which is a method used by many professionals to understand and prevent for example incidents. Root cause analysis is a critical tool in these cases. You use it to drill down until you get to the core causes, asking questions that are data-driven. However, save the 'why' for situations and cases, not for dealing with people.

Asking questions that focus on what happened rather than why someone did something tend to be more revealing and are rarely perceived as accusatory. Questions such as, 'What could have been done differently? What was the earliest point that you understood the project was going to be delayed? Who was involved?' will lead to solid answers and solutions. The table below lists questions to avoid and their replacement counterparts.

DON'T SAY (AVOID WHY AND YOU AND CLOSED QUESTIONS)	DO SAY (USE WHO, WHAT, WHERE, WHEN, HOW, ME, US, WE, AND OPEN QUESTIONS)
Why did you do that?	How did you decide to do that?
What *were* you thinking?	Take me through the steps leading up to what happened.
On what planet is this a good idea?	How did this come about?
How could you let this happen?	What do you think happened?
Did you think this was a good idea/plan/decision?	Where did this come from?
Are you sure you're proud of what you've produced?	What might have prevented this from occurring? or How could we have prevented this?
Would anyone else think this was a good report/project/plan/delivery?	What would this need to look like to get it approved/supported? What would a successful delivery look like?
Should you have done this?	What alternatives could have been helpful/useful to do?
Was this really necessary?	
Are you always going to be late, deliver badly, etc.?	Where could you find help to get this finished?
If it's not your fault, whose is it?	What other priorities need tending to before this?
Why can't you be more like X?	When can I expect this delivery?
You couldn't come up with anything else?	What gets in the way of being on time?
Are you serious?	How can we figure out where this went wrong and what to do about it?
Are you just being difficult?	Who could help you to get this on track?
Could you be less negative?	What additional ideas/suggestions can you consider?
	What solutions do you see might work here?
	If we take a look at what's possible—what ideas do we open up for?

What's more, whilst your conversation may be one-on-one, don't kill the messenger. It might well be that the issue lies in how you, as a leader, presented the task, clarity or lack thereof in your expectations, assumptions that were not explicitly discussed, lack of trust in the relationship, so the other party didn't feel comfortable coming back to you for support earlier in the process or lack of follow up on your part. The main difference between responsibility and accountability is that responsibility can be shared whilst accountability cannot. As the leader, you are always accountable for whether the various responsibilities within your team are achieved as executed. Rarely is only one person responsible for any outcome and asking the right questions can lead to improved mutual understanding and to a collaborative resolution.

BUT OUT

The most common way we invalidate even the best attempt at collaborating is by saying 'Yes...but'. Once the but has arrived in the conversation, it basically says that what was said before was not really valid, and you're going to correct or refer to something better. No doubt you'll have heard or used yourself phrases such as 'You did a great job there but...' or 'I like that idea but...' or 'I agree with you but...' or 'That will probably work but...' If you want to add to someone else's idea, move on from their point or show a different, perhaps conflicting perspective. Use AND instead. This is at the heart of what organisational coaches and psychologists use in change management approaches called Appreciative Inquiry. AI attempts to use ways of asking questions and envisioning the future in order to foster positive relationships and build on the present potential of a given person, organisation or situation. It focuses on identifying what is working well, analysing why it is working well, and then doing more of it.

DIG DEEPER: THE FOUR D MODEL

For a deeper understanding of the Four D model approach to AI, see 'The Theory of Appreciative Inquiry' developed by David Cooperrider and Suresh Srivastva in a paper they published in 1986.[28] In their thesis, they offer a collaborative, strengths-based approach to change in organisations and other human systems described as follows:

'Appreciative inquiry methodology and initiatives are the specific techniques and operational steps that are used to bring about positive change in a system'. The Four Ds are:

- Discover—Appreciating and valuing the best of What Is. Here, information and stories are gathered about what is working well.

---

28   D. L. Cooperrider, Srivastva, S. 'Appreciative inquiry in organizational life'. In Woodman, R. W. & Pasmore, W.A. (eds.). *Research in Organizational Change and Development*. Vol. 1. Stamford, CT: JAI Press. pp. 129–169, 1987.

- Dream—Envisioning What Might Be.
- Design—Determining What Should Be.
- Deliver (or Destiny)—Innovating What Will Be.

A fifth D was added later by practitioners to the beginning of the Four D process and refers to the earliest necessary stage, i.e., 'Define' what the focus is and what needs to be addressed.

The key differences between AI and problem-focused approaches lie in how you phrase your questions or enquiry to explore positively. Problem-solving asks, 'What's wrong and how do we fix it?' The problem and its root cause are analysed to develop a plan of action. Appreciative inquiry, instead, asks, 'What's working and how do we do it?' The approach looks at the situation 'as is' without judgment and imagines an ideal situation to create a positive outcome. Solutions are developed collaboratively.

SOCRATIC QUESTIONING STYLE

You may know Socrates as a philosopher. Philosophy, by its nature, asks questions, looking for meaning and understanding of life. Socratic questioning then uses questions to search for meaning and understanding.

Socrates posed six types of questions:

1. Clarifying concepts:	How does this relate to the topic/or the goal?
	What models might you use to explain your ideas?
2. Questions that probe assumptions:	What else might be an explanation for this?
	What is the evidence for this conclusion?
3. Questions that probe reasons and evidence:	Can you give me a concrete example?
	What business priority is this built on/or aligned with?
4. Questions about viewpoints and perspectives:	If we looked at it from the stakeholder's perspective, what would be important then?
	What would be an alternative explanation?
5. Questions that probe implications and consequences:	What impact will this have on the rest of the business?
	What are the consequences of that reasoning?
6. Questions about the question:	What was behind that question?
	What did you hear/understand/take away when I asked that question?

In leadership, Socratic questioning of what something means to an individual helps you understand motivation. You can use Socratic questioning to find the hook. For example, you may be working on a project with an employee who feels pressured by the workload or worried about their performance, and they're looking for reassurance and feedback. Through Socratic questioning, you delve into the employee's concerns and when you ask what the workload means to them, you discover they are worried about quality being compromised. At that point, your role as a leader might be to see what is available to support them, rearrange priorities or simply reassure them how competent they are, and help them go into any future encounters with that empowered frame of mind. Assure them that you believe in them.

Socrates asked: what does an experience mean to you? There is no truth in experience; there is only experience. The value lies in what it means.

CURIOUS QUESTIONING

Literature about staying curious is proliferate. The innovation rhetoric encourages experimentation and curiosity about doing things differently. Everyone nowadays is talking about digitalisation, automation, improving efficiency, reducing waste and unnecessary activity.

Whilst curious questioning is a great tool to stimulate innovation, it is also extremely useful for conflict resolution. When people feel threatened or criticised, becoming defensive is a natural reaction. They make statements to defend themselves. Curious questioning is a brilliant way to remain offensive and look for data that can be disputed or countered with facts that will move the conversation or situation past the point of conflict.

DIG DEEPER: AN INVITATION TO CURIOSITY

G. Cecchin, in an article titled 'Hypothesizing, circularity, and neutrality revisited: An invitation to curiosity,' articulated the notion of curiosity as the fundamental aspirational position a therapist ought to adopt when working with a family.[29] Neutrality and curiosity are interlinked, as neutrality creates a state of curiosity that 'leads to exploration of alternate views…with a concomitant nonattachment to a particular position'.

For example, after a meeting, if you get feedback that someone felt you were hostile or aggressive towards them when they put their point of view across, the natural tendency may be to say, 'That's just the way I am. That's not what I meant. I think you read the wrong intentions.' Instead, try saying, 'I'm curious about that. What about me did you notice that you thought was aggressive or dismissive?'

The other person may respond that it was your tone of voice, or maybe you were loud, or you looked directly at them. You may decide you need to own that and apologise, reassuring them it wasn't about them. You may have been criticised by a leader before you came into the room, which made you feel blamed, so you reacted

---

29   G. Cecchin, 'Hypothesizing, circularity, and neutrality revisited: An invitation to curiosity,' *Fam Process*, 26(4):405-13, 1987.

aggressively and inappropriately in the meeting. Or you were sensitive to what you had to do, and others misread your body language when you entered the room. Perhaps you were just unaware.

FOUR BUMS ON A BENCH

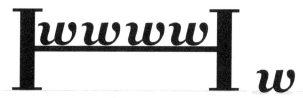

(Adapted from Rudyard Kipling: "I Keep Six Honest Serving Men")

Ask Who, What, When, Where, and How of someone's actions; reserve Why for situations.

When I give presentations about PIN, this graphic always gets a laugh from the audience, yet it provides an easy way to remember the questions that drive curious questioning: Who, What, When, and Where, which sit on the bench of How, whilst Why is excluded—you'll notice the last 'bum' is kicked off the bench because it's unfriendly. Remember: why is unfriendly toward people, but great for situations.

Curious questions are an opportunity for the other person to share useful feedback and for you to have a better understanding of yourself. It keeps you in learning mode by providing you with data and relates to the ladder of inference discussed earlier.

INVESTIGATIVE QUESTIONING

Investigative questioning is a more formal technique and useful in digging into details, looking into gaps in data, facts, evidence, seeing the holes in the picture or specific argumentation, testing hypotheses, eliciting contradictions for resolution, critiquing biases and assumptions, exploring links between data sets or ideas. Investigative questioning may be one-sided, be linear in its form and feel much like a Q&A. Closed and open questions to explore and confirm ideas are used in tandem typically in structured processes, for example, investigation into an incident, product/concept pressure-testing or forward planning an event. If you've ever been interviewed by the police, you may have experienced this type of questioning—it can feel direct, straight to the point, short in tempo, and functional (i.e., serving an explicitly agreed purpose) or it may feel as though it's attempting to get under your skin, so to speak, feeling invasive and long in tempo where the person continues to ask for more and more information to the point of discomfort.

In the opening example of the senior leader who dominated the meeting, she frequently used a more investigative method of questioning to make sure the team stays on track and obtains the right data at the right time in the right way. It was felt to be interrogative as it went on too long or was aimed at a single member of the team. Its usefulness predominantly lies in either incident investigation or as a check-and-balance approach to a final decision to ensure all key factors or aspects have been covered before moving forward. In dialogue with people, this approach should be avoided unless served upfront with clear purpose as a formal question-and-answer type dialogue. If you've ever had that feeling that someone is intense or overstepping boundaries with you in their questions when you meet, it's possible they are using an investigative approach in the wrong context or are using it clumsily to build the relationship through soliciting more knowledge. This approach is for formal situations and not for day-to-day, trust-building relations. Leaders should be clear about this difference.

The use of language has changed so much over time and is so culturally specific. But the core tenets of questioning have largely remained unchanged based on the founding figures in psychiatry, psychology and philosophical curiosity. We give them different spins and new titles, but fundamentally as humans, we haven't evolved that much when it comes to the way we structure our values and beliefs, even if the values and beliefs themselves may change over time as we're exposed to different social influences and advances in technology, which gives us new ideas.

TONE OF VOICE

Perhaps the most influential aspect of what we say is *how* we say it and that comes down to tone of voice.

We use voice tone, inflexion and emphasis every day in how we attempt to convey what we mean, seek clarifications, ask questions, make statements, give opinions, etc.

Take an example of being asked if you could offer a greater salary to an employee—and you know you can't, so you might say it with a firm tone of voice indicating there is no room for flexibility or negotiation here. On the other hand, if you end the statement with an inflexion as we do in questions—it may infer that you are not 100 per cent fixed on your position and there is room for further discussion.

Tone of voice has a significant impact on others—it reveals beyond the words what you might be feeling, or underlying intentions. Having congruence between the words and the tone of voice conveys integrity and empathy when it also is in harmony with the other party. There are other aspects to tone of voice that may be less under our conscious control—for example, pitch and depth. Margaret Thatcher, the first woman Prime Minister in Britain in the 1980s, famously used voice coaches to train her to lower her voice to a slower, more measured firmer quality and very slightly deeper. Research tells us that deeper, slower voices are considered more authoritative, calm and overall more controlled than shrill and faster ones.[30] Whilst it would be quite odd to start lowering your voice artificially for a conversation with someone, it might be worth watching yourself on video giving a presentation or in a meeting, for example, to see if you are expressing yourself calmly and with appropriate control or whether slowing it down (which will naturally slightly deepen the voice)—may be of benefit in getting your message across effectively.

OPEN SHARING VERSUS BRUTAL HONESTY

The necessity of complete openness in leadership is a myth, and at times, being overly open can damage a leader's reputation and diminish his respect by his team. Some will say if you're in a bad mood, you should share your emotions with your team to show you're not a robot. In leadership, before baring your soul, you need to ask yourself why you are sharing. Ask yourself if there is learning or a benefit. If there's a benefit to the other person to know that you're in a bad mood because they will be able to do something about it, or it's a learning opportunity for them, then sharing would be beneficial. If it's only about

30   Barbara Borkowska, Janie Johnson, Marta Kowal, Anna Oleszkiewicz, Katarzyna Pisanski, David A Puts, Agnieszka Sorokowska, Piotr Sorokowski, Olga Zólkiewicz, 'Voice of Authority: Professionals Lower Their Vocal Frequencies When Giving Expert Advice', *Journal of Nonverbal Behavior,* May 2019. https://www.researchgate.net/publication/332915511_Voice_of_ Authority_Professionals_Lower_Their_Vocal_Frequencies_When_Giving_Expert_Advice.

getting something off your chest because it will make you feel better, do it in private somewhere else. The sharing isn't about you; it has to be about the impact on other people. The content can be personal rather than private, which ensures openness with exposure and should be helpful to others in understanding why you might, for example, need more time, change priorities or be less available than usual.

So, what can you do? If you had a particularly bad encounter and you're going straight into another meeting afterwards, you could be better prepared by informing people in the second meeting that you need ten minutes to yourself before beginning. You're not obligated to share why you need those ten minutes, and at times sharing is detrimental. If the team knows you're struggling, every time you challenge something they bring up, they might chalk it off to your bad mood. They won't take you seriously.

LANGUAGE MIRRORING

Mirroring body language has been addressed already, but here we discuss mirroring consciously with words as the key to expressing empathy. As evidenced throughout the stories in the book, people are not asking for your physical presence in and of itself; they want to be understood, valued and recognised. Mirroring what people say affirms what you heard and is one of the most powerful influencing techniques in expressing empathy.

For example, two colleagues are speaking together. One shares that they've had a bad encounter and felt misunderstood and misrepresented. They may say they want to vent and talk it through. In mirroring, the listener responds that he hears and understand what they're saying. He then reflects back with a summary statement, such as, 'That probably felt awful when you were shut down whilst presenting your viewpoint and they all turned away from you when you spoke.'

Mirroring in conversation is powerful because you affirm for the other person that you heard what they said. You evidence that by repeating it back in a summary—not word for word—providing them with the opportunity to correct or recalibrate what you heard.

Mirroring is linked to affirmative statements. The affirmative statements may not be directly summarising or reflective, but they will affirm that you are listening and have understood. Counsellors are classically trained in the art of empathic mirroring through statements in dialogue. They will summarise in words what the other party has said to show that they have listened carefully. Reflect that back to them and check that they have understood accurately. They will use statements to convey that such as, 'If I understood you correctly—what you said was...' Or 'Let me check I have understood what you need/mean/want.' This offers an opportunity for the counsellor to check out their takeaways and seek further clarifications if needed, or to neutralise assumptions. The result is that this mirroring of what has been said is the explicit evidence of empathy or active listening. This transfers very easily to leadership dialogues with team members on task clarifications or conflicts but also to stakeholder conversations when trying to elicit support through understanding their needs or perspectives.

Mirroring especially works well when you link to the other person's NLP mode. If they are auditory, you might say, 'That sounds like a great plan.' Whereas, if they are visual, you may say, 'It looks like you are doing a great job.' And, if they are kinesthetic: 'When you say that, it feels good.'

DEALING WITH RESISTANCE AND PUSHBACK

Curiosity and the Ladder of Inference will be two of your best options when you reach a standoff or face pushback and resistance to your agenda.

For instance, if somebody is pushing back and saying they're not budging on price on a contract or service offering, you would go into quite specific questions around the basis of their position. Start from the top of the Ladder of

Inference and invite them to share data, criteria, facts and details that will help to get down a rung or two and steer away from taking positions. You also should be prepared to share yours.

When you're dealing with resistance and pushback and can't come to an agreement or persuade the other person to your argument, remember the tips from great influencers and negotiators. Validate and strengthen your position by providing credible proof in the form of data or citations, i.e., 'This is what our competitors do, or I have another offer which is X.' Likewise, if they say something that you don't believe or agree with, ask them for credible sources or what benchmark they're using. Seek evidence that backs up their position. With their explanation, you can then counter a solution or response.

If facing a situation with a noncooperative colleague or resistance from a team member, coming from a place of curiosity will help by exploring the issue from both sides of the table to try to understand each other's needs. Open up the possibility that one of you has misunderstood or not fully explained something. Invite people to envision what they need first—seek their interests and find common ground.

Pushback and resistance come from being self-absorbed in one's own interests. The moment you get out of that self-absorbed mode and get curious, you can open up for what you may have in common with the other party.

When someone resists, it's usually because they're not seeing the common ground with you. In business, looking for common ground might require raising your joint perspective one level up to the department goals. For instance, if you're both in the same department and you must work together to deliver a project but have differing views on prioritising this amongst everything else you have to do, you might look for the common ground, i.e., where are we both connected to this task? Is it a goal at the department or business unit level you both belong to so that it affects the overall team's performance rating for example, and if so, what do you need to do to reach that goal? There may be a reciprocity option, 'You help me now, and I'll have time to help you later.' Suddenly you're no longer on opposite sides of the table. You are both on the same side working towards a goal but with different pressures. That shared point of view can often crack the impasse.

You can also use third-party observation. If you perhaps brought in the imagined perspective of the senior vice president from business development (a key stakeholder in your work) into your conversation, what would they expect or advise? Shifting perspectives based on different viewpoints can help to see situations more clearly and provide new insights into ways forward. In psychology, this is similar to what is called bringing your internal supervisor in, the voice of reason that you've learned through working with somebody like a mentor or coach and imagining what they might ask or say.

Consider also if you are guilty of the kind of issue you are raising with the other person. Are you being stubborn and inflexible, controlling or lost in the details? Ask yourself if you are modelling the behaviour yourself. Entitled leaders do not ask this question of themselves often enough and point to everybody else, but are not paying attention to themselves. Feedback should be about helping the other person, but it requires you to practise what you preach.

FEEDBACK

On the topic of feedback, ask before you give it. You are not entitled to give feedback, although it is a necessary part of the development of yourself and others. Approach and timing is key. Even though you have the role of leader, the feedback will be better received if you ask the person if they're ready to hear it. They may not be. If they say no, take that to mean that you're on opposite sides of the table, and you will want to explore that. Ask what they are concerned about that you might share when you offer feedback. Or, if today is simply not a good day to hear the feedback due to other background pressures.

You don't need to be brutal. It isn't about you sharing to feel better but about the receiver learning.

Giving feedback is about the other person's interest in hearing feedback as much as your interest in sharing. Leaders are encouraged to be their true, authentic selves. We want people to have integrity in their values as leaders, but brutal honesty and nonconstructive criticism is unhelpful and will create a defensive response in the other party, meaning they will be less likely to listen to what you are saying or take your feedback as credible or valid. Leaders must communicate filtered, respectful authenticity. We often forget that our co-workers are not obliged to make the same allowances for our behaviour as our family is. If your default is to be brutal and honest, it may not be appreciated. Use the platinum rule as your guide and give feedback in the manner the listener wants to hear it. Frame it with a positive solution-focused opportunity if possible, like with AI, you might focus on what you'd like to see more of than what went wrong. So, asking the person to be more punctual for meetings is better than asking them to stop being late.

With respect to receiving feedback, the engaged leader will be more open to listening to this than the entitled. The leader will be curious as to the basis for the feedback and if it is negative and/or creates feelings of anger or resistance, then will use the Ladder of Inference to gather data and information. The most important starting point is to thank the other person for offering you that gift of feedback—it will have taken some courage if they are a subordinate to be that open with you. Secondly, acknowledge that you will reflect on what you have heard and come back to them with what you have decided to do with it. Then do just that. Remember that reliability, consistency, and predictability are important characteristics of a trusted leader.

THE USE OF SILENCE AND INTERRUPTION

Whilst C stands for conversation, keep in mind that silence isn't necessarily silent. Silence can be a welcome invitation for people to open up and give more or perhaps deeper information. Clinical psychologists and psychotherapists know the power of silence in dialogue perhaps more than most. The first phase of silence offers people the opportunity to think, reflect and raise issues because it gives rise to subconscious thoughts.

At a certain point, silence enters a second phase, which causes discomfort. We've all had that experience of a long gap or a pregnant pause. There's a natural tendency for most people to want to fill the silence at this point. Savvy leaders hone the skills to tolerate the uncomfortable point. The leader can be well-served, particularly in challenging or difficult conversations, to wait and allow the other person to speak further. It is during the second, uncomfortable phase of silence that people often share more or useful information, which might not have been readily shared otherwise. Of course, silence will never get people to say things they didn't want to say, but it does give them the space to say it at a time when they hadn't necessarily planned to or allows them to build the momentum or confidence to do so.

Uncomfortable silence can be filled with the tangible feeling of words left unsaid. You can sense the ether between the two people when the silence communicates unexpressed feelings or emotion. Skilled leaders can pick up on visual cues and behaviour, observing a furrowed brow or concerned look on the person's face. They can explore that silence with empathetic observations such as, 'I feel that you're not very happy,' or 'What are you feeling when I say this to you', encouraging the person to share.

Besides the lack of words, silence itself is a great data provider. It should not be rescued or resolved without due thought. The speaker who breaks the silence should consider: if I'm going to fill the silence, what am I going to fill it with? Is it better for the other person to fill it, because they may well need to say something or share something that's of value?

Yet, not all silences are empty spaces needing to be filled.

Some silences are peaceful and reflective, like meditation, or listening without speaking. Silence can, at times, be comfortable, like the feeling you have when sitting in silence with someone you know very well. Silent reflection is an underused tool by most leaders. It is an opportunity to take stock for example at the start of the day, pondering on what the day holds, how to prioritise, or using it for visualised rehearsal of forthcoming meetings or presentations.

The counterpart to silence is interruption. I've seen few leaders use interruption skilfully or gracefully. The principle is the same as that for feedback: you want your interruptions to be meaningful and useful. If you're interrupting to get something off your chest or share a point, you may not be listening and are instead making a selfish interruption to satisfy the urge to say something.

You can tell when interruption lacks skill or mutual purpose as it's often at odds with either the emotion or content the other person is sharing. You can see a physical reaction in the other person that this interruption was meaningless or didn't connect to what was being shared. And so, interruption is most valuable for a leader when, for example, the conversation is going off track and if done skilfully, will be readily accepted by the other person, often with an apology once they realise they've gone off track.

An interruption might be useful to break up a conflictual dialogue between two other people. The way you interrupt is important. You can lead into your interruption with something that gives you permission to enter the conversation. For example, if the interruption is required between you and another person because the conversation is off track, you can say, 'Okay, I've noticed that but we're now drifting away from the topic that we were here to discuss.' or 'I realise that we're running out of time, and I think we need to get back to the key issue on the table.' You acknowledge the other person and label the purpose of the interruption up front to give them a context to understand your interruption, rather than jumping in with 'What I was trying to say...' or simply coughing loudly or waving hands in the air to silence them.

If you're going to interrupt two people, you become the observer, and say, 'Perhaps we could take a step back and see if we're having the conversation we need to be having and addressing the right points.' You remain in curious mode rather than telling mode.

DIG DEEPER: FREUD'S SILENCE

Freud, in his psychotherapy sessions, would keep the session time to fifty minutes, not an hour. The extra ten minutes in the hour before his next session was presumably pragmatic and used for the purpose of writing notes.[31] The time-length was theorised after the fact, psychotherapists believing that it created a discipline for the patient to share what they wished within the firm boundaries for that fifty minutes—to use the time effectively. Long reflective silences were commonplace, allowing the patient to reveal more through the unconscious rising to the surface. Freud noted that patients frequently waited until the end of their session to mention the most emotionally revealing material presumably because it is difficult to talk about. They wanted the therapist to know, but they didn't feel able to tolerate a discussion around it, so they leave it with them.

Like Freud, set a definite time-length for a conversation or meeting and be disciplined about keeping it, then pay attention to words, silences and not only what's raised at the beginning, but what's raised at the very end. How are you left feeling? What is the person leaving you with? What is the message they're giving you?

For an easy read and overview of the use of silence in therapeutic contexts, read: 'Compassionate Silence in the Patient–Clinician Encounter: A Contemplative Approach'.[32]

RULES OF ENGAGEMENT

So, we see from the above that the language of influential

---

31   Herbert Will, 'The Concept of the 50-Minute Hour: Time forming a frame for the unconscious', *International Forum of Psychoanalysis,* January 10, 2018.

32   Anthony L. Back, M.D., et al, 'Compassionate silence in the patient-clinician encounter: a contemplative approach', *J Palliat Med,* 12(12):1113-7, 2009.

leadership lies predominantly in questions, rather than statements, and in use of reflective silence. Conversation is as much about what you don't say as what you do, and how you use space and silence to allow others to contribute. Speaking last in an open discussion within a team is often a great idea for a leader. You pull the information together rather than push it, using open questions: who, what, where, when, how, tell me more. As a leader, you want to harvest the best out of the group you're leading without railroading them into your way of thinking and closing down for new inputs or ideas.

Great teams can self-manage and self-steer because they know each other well and have built a lot of trust—we talk about how they do that in chapter two. If they've worked together a long time, they usually have established conscious shared agreements and rules of engagement, which reflect the culture of the team.

You'll want to establish the rules of engagement for your team—often referred to as Ground Rules or Team Charters. These refer to shared agreements on how you will engage and contribute to discussions and expectations you have to each other in the team, ideas around what respect looks like for this team, how you express and tolerate disagreement, how and where decisions are made, punctuality, preparations, etc., so that every team has its own characteristics for what is accepted and the norms in engaging with each other. Many a leadership team process begins with establishing this set of guidelines with the team, particularly when the team is new or has one or two new members. Making explicit the expectations to behaviour and conversation as well as cooperation and collaboration will save you countless hours in conflict mediation or addressing poor performance further down the line. Specifically, a good place to start is in meetings, whether you're meeting with one person or a team. At the beginning, identify your common agenda and the outcome you seek. Decide where you want to be at the end of the forty-five-minute meeting you're about to have and start the conversation from there.

APPLY A TO C

As a leader, in your preparation, think about the conversation you're going to have. Think about asking about the difficult issues a little earlier, making sure you give that helpful space and silence for the other person to respond. Consider ahead of time how the conversation may go and how you'll respond in different scenarios. For example, how do you address the employee or colleague who cries during a disclosure or conversation? The natural reflex might be to spontaneously hug them as you might a friend, not always an appropriate response in today's business world perhaps. How can you make someone feel hugged, supported and cared for without physically hugging them? Use silence balanced by validating and empathic words such as 'It's okay to be upset. Take your time. Don't worry. I'm not judging you.' Allow the person to express themselves without trying to rescue the space or close their emotion down.

I attended a leadership team development where the facilitator asked his team members to share an early defining experience that had impacted their leadership today. The first woman in the room shared about her divorce and welled up. She said the experience had made her much more empathic as a leader, and she was able to think about the importance of understanding personal situations and their impact on work performance. The second leader told a similar story about her parents' divorce. I noticed the leader starting to roll his eyes.

Another shared the sudden, unexpected death of his father when young and how that experience taught him resilience and independence. Others who didn't know that about him were quite shocked, and there were a few tearing eyes.

As the fourth person got ready to speak, the leader said, 'Here we go, another sob story.' Awkward laughter spread through the room as it was said jokingly, but it was incredibly invalidating for the next person. The leader closed down the space for that kind of conversation.

The leader knew he was coming into an environment where people would be asked to share personal stories. He should have prepared better for his tolerance and ability to bear both the content and the space required for that.

As you prepare for what could be a difficult or vulnerable meeting, create a plan for your dialogue and facilitation that allows space and breathing time for the conversation. Use what's in the room: space, time, silence to remain authentic and empathic.

THE VITAL TAKEAWAY

Learning and using different styles of questions to steer a conversation can seem manipulative. In truth, it goes back to the A of approach. Stay in curious mode and get to know the person or group to whom you're speaking as well as you can. You can then determine the questioning style that will be most effective. Remember the platinum rule: it's not about how you'd like to deliver the message but how the receiver would like to hear the message. Consider the tone of voice you use when you ask and respond to questions. Remember to be consistent in your behaviour (as discussed in chapter four) and your words.

A person feels valued, validated, understood, and motivated when you find their hook or identify with their interests. You can be conscious of validating them not from the way you feel, but in the way that works best for them.

We already do this with children as part of healthy, positive parenting. Instead of telling them they did a great job building a tower, for instance, you might compliment their effort and how hard they worked because you want to validate the person, not the goal. When they do something you ask of them, you compliment how they listened, not that the work itself was great. You allow room for failure, but you celebrate efforts.

To be clear, you are not practising the ABC method to gain something for you alone at the cost of the other person. You're doing it to support your PIN, help the other person and provide the information in the way that they want it served.

Think of reciprocity and the idea of servant leadership. When you are motivated by the question of what the other needs from you so they can do their job in the best possible way, that's not manipulation; that's serving.

We've now covered A, B, and C singly. In the next chapter, let's look at how they work together in typical workplace scenarios and how honing ABC skills moves the needle towards engaged leader on the leadership spectrum.

CHAPTER 6

✳ ✳ ✳

BRINGING IT ALL TOGETHER

We rarely thoroughly plan our approach, behaviour or conversation for interactions with people we've known and collaborated with successfully for a long time. The preparation occurs albeit subconsciously and quite naturally in the course of an encounter. We exchange ideas, we lean in and mirror behaviour, we express empathy, and reach a win-win conclusion. It can happen in simple conversations about deciding which restaurant to go to for lunch or in more weighty discussions such as choosing between two candidates for a new position.

ABC becomes a conscious effort when you know someone less well when there are several levels between you and the other person within the hierarchy, and you need to influence where you don't have mandate or authority, or when you simply don't get along with the other person, yet are required to collaborate.

You might recall the challenges leaders face that were discussed in chapter two—maybe you even recognised some of those challenges as your own. I promised to provide a framework as easy as ABC to address those challenges, and in the three previous chapters, tools for Approach, Behaviour and Conversation have been presented separately. In practise, however, they are quite inseparable and work together fluidly as you'll see in the scenarios in this closing chapter. Some of the best learning happens by example, and so presented here are six common workplace situations to illustrate effective use of ABC.

In each scenario, we find an engaged leader preparing his or her approach, behaviour and conversation in anticipation of an interaction with another leader or group. The engaged leader is doing everything right, whilst the other party may be less aware of ABC. As you read the stories, you'll likely identify with parts of all the players— as mentioned, all leaders fall somewhere on the spectrum between entitled and engaged leader. Think of these stories as a mirror to what you're doing well and to reflect any of your behaviours that could use improvement.

At the end of each story, you'll find a list of the tools used by the engaged leader, so if you want to refresh your memory, you can go back and review the specific tool in the previous chapters.

SCENARIO 1: THE COLLABORATIVE PROJECT

Thoughtful consideration begins when you send out a meeting invitation and decide who should attend and through to how you structure the meeting and the content you include. Meetings executed with quality, i.e., efficiency and clear purpose, with open possibility of harvesting contributions from the others, are a mark of team leadership where work done is only that which can be achieved by coming together. Many an ineffective meeting is a gathering simply to share information that could have been shared more efficiently in other ways ahead of the gathering. Doing that and then using the team time for sharing perspectives, or planning actions is a far better use of the members' time and resources.

Some of the biggest challenges in business arise during joint collaborations, which may occur across teams, departments, silos or businesses. Whether the project is between internal players across silos, for example, reorganising internally or building a new business unit, or an external project such as a joint venture, the investment of time and resources is often sizable. At the beginning of the project, the partners may not know each other very well. Starting the relationship in a positive, cooperative manner sets the tone for the experience over the life of the project. Although each party is a partner in the project, one tends to be the natural or appointed lead, whilst all parties work toward a common goal or win-win solution. Let's look at how collaborative influence works in practise.

Consider the case of Preeti and John, two leaders from different companies who are collaborating on a large construction project. John's company is leading the project. Preeti's becoming increasingly aware that the project is likely to miss milestone deadlines but doesn't have concrete information about the workload and timelines. The project's success or lack thereof will have significant consequences for both companies. She's concerned about the costs associated with the overruns, and whether the project will break even, let alone be profitable. John and Preeti have met several times in previous project meetings. Preeti believes John is a bit conflict-shy, not revealing his concerns about the project to avoid stressing the relationship between their two companies and criticising his team. Surely, he's aware of and concerned about the risk of missed deadlines and loss, but her impression is that he's not willing to name the elephants in the room when the team meets at the discussion table. Preeti feels that for the project to be successful for all involved parties, someone needs to expose what's going on and name it.

Preeti wants John to trust her enough to share what he

feels about the project and enable her to be the voice in the room, albeit that she's not the leader of the project. She wants to reassure John that she is an ally and her actions are for the success of the project, which creates a win-win situation for both their companies.

Shortly before a joint meeting, Preeti approaches John in the hallway and opens the conversation with small talk, and as they approach the meeting room, asks how he feels about the upcoming meeting.

John shares that he believes it will be a good meeting and mentions having some concerns about ensuring they address the right issues. As soon as Preeti hears the word concern, she asks about them.

This was exactly the type of information that she was looking for. Preeti had done her homework about John's company and the issues on the project before this meeting and had reason to believe they had unspoken concerns about the delays. She knew which player held the information she sought, but she also knew he was cagey about revealing his concerns. She had thought about her approach ahead of time and was ready to respond in a way that seemed spontaneous yet was actually prepared.

John broadly expresses his concerns that there have been some delays already. Preeti validates what she heard, mirroring his comments and expressing curiosity about the feelings he'd shared, rather than drilling deeper at this point.

John reveals a bit more. He explains the delays have not been followed up with the sub-contractor thoroughly, and Preeti again validates what he said and then asks deeper questions as to who has responsibility for that and the earliest date that they can expect to have that done by.

She used the circular technique to gather facts and data. She opened with a broad question that sounded like small talk and was an artful invitation to dialogue. She then picked up on key phrases or words the other leader used to drill down to another layer of information. Because she first validated what John said, he didn't feel like he was being interrogated.

Her questions were never confrontational and instead involving. She used words such as 'we', 'mutual interest', and 'in this together'.

By the time they'd reached the end of the hallway, she'd garnered quite a bit of data about the subcontractors being the likely cause of delay and cost overruns. More importantly, she'd created an alliance with John. When they entered the meeting room, they carried on the natural flow of their dialogue. They poured coffee for each other. She'd built rapport. When they sat at the table, they sat at the corner of the table and near to each other—when partners from different sides of the project team usually sit directly across from each other.

Once the conversation started in the meeting, she was able to naturally raise questions, asking about how the project was being followed up, make points that referred to the concerns raised without revealing that he had shared the information. She made casual eye contact with her new ally, who nodded in agreement. She was able to push a little bit further and deeper without being confrontational. Preeti was able to voice the concerns that John was reticent to express.

During the entire conversation, she used a calm, exploratory tone of voice, never stressed or accusatory. She used the 'bums on a bench' questions to avoid asking why and attributing blame such as, 'What was the process for follow up of the contractors? Who was responsible for that? How was the schedule and cost profile looking today? When would the subcontractors actually deliver? Where did the risks now lie? How could we all ensure a timely and cost effective final delivery on the project?'

The activities and conversations before the meeting are the icebreakers, the relationship connectors that give data on interests to find a win-win. Far from exploiting John for information, Preeti explored common ground in their interests for the project to be profitable, delivered on time and successful for both of their companies.

Building rapport outside the meeting room enables the conversation to continue after entering the room. Through these interactions, trust builds, which is especially important in situations like this where the relationship is long-term.

Your leadership role may not always be to lead a project directly but to contribute to the leadership of a project through consulting or collaborative efforts. To secure success in this case, you have to nurture and maintain the relationship and build trust. Preeti used empathic behaviours that contributed to building knowledge of and understanding each other.

WHAT WAS IN PLAY:

- Approach—stakeholder and project analysis, understanding interests, knowing the personal style
- Behaviour—mirroring, empathic body language, seating
- Conversation—circular questioning, 'bums on a bench' question, and empathic tone of voice

SCENARIO 2: THE UNLIKEABLE COLLEAGUE

Let's be honest. There's a strange expectation that leaders should like everyone with whom they work. Yet, we all have people we don't like for one reason or another, that one colleague who rubs everyone the wrong way. Often the reason we don't like each other is because we don't know each other very well. If the first time we meet someone, they're having a bad day because their car was sideswiped on the way to work, we have an instant reaction to their bad mood and may assume they're a negative person. We then bring that assumption with us each time we bump into the person. At some point, we might learn that they carry a heavy load in their personal life, making work a lower priority and affecting their engagement.

Jane got along with everyone in the office, but then there was David. David was another project leader of a small team in their company who had wanted to lead the project Jane was in charge of. However, she'd been selected to be responsible instead of him. Now, given his role in the IT department, she had realised he needed to be consulted and kept informed on the project Jane was leading. Jane had noticed that every time there was a challenge to solve, he'd recount how he'd solved an unrelated problem twenty years ago at a famous startup where he'd been employee number six, touting his expansive knowledge and previous experience. For a long time, Jane was never sure why David worked for the present company, since neither the products, the company nor the people ever seemed to live up to his past experience. She recently learned at one of the social gatherings after work that David had left the last job after fifteen years of seeing others hired in above him. He felt he should have been the leader because he'd been there from the beginning, but the founders and board didn't view him in that capacity. He'd been hired as a contributor and remained a contributor. Jane knew David had good qualities, but his personality was just so irritating.

But, they had to work together, and Jane often needed David's input for her project on the technical side where he had the expertise that she didn't, though he seemed to enjoy seeing her struggle if only to prove a point that she wasn't competent enough to lead the project. She knew she needed to draw on her empathy to garner David's collaboration.

Dreading having to ask him for his help and being turned down or expecting him to go on about his competence and experience, Jane continually avoided setting up a meeting with David. One Thursday morning, she was walking to the breakroom and just as she rounded the corner of the open-plan office area, she saw David approaching from the other direction.

Her brow furrowed and her shoulders tensed. She paused.

She needed to have that difficult conversation. She considered turning around and going back to her desk without her caffeine fix.

Instead, she decided to change her mindset and stay open to having a better encounter with him this time. What could she do? She adopted opposite behaviour, dropping her shoulders and smiling to herself. In the fifteen seconds it took to reach the room, she prepared what she'd say in a way that David would be open to hearing.

In previous meetings, David often responded with feelings such as, 'I don't feel that's the right way to go', or 'I sense this is the wrong approach', or 'I feel this is more complex than you realise' despite her attempts to sway him with hard facts. Jane concluded that he was a kinesthetic listener and learner, so he'd been more receptive to her question whilst he was pouring himself a cup of coffee and if she appealed to his feelings of authority and competence. She hooked into his interest to be recognised for his experience and need to feel special on this project; he couldn't refuse the opportunity to shine.

Jane smiled as she greeted David and moved her cup closer to his, keeping him busy whilst she asked if they could meet later that afternoon to discuss the project. 'Hi, David, how's your day going? I wondered if I could ask you to help me, given your experience with this issue I'm having on the project—you'd be the best person to advise me on the technical risks for the project?' Her tone of voice soft and curious, using inflexion to give him the signal she was open to his reply to her question. He agreed without resorting to his usual diatribe of past experience. She'd named it up front, validated it and appealed to his interest and motivation to be seen as the expert. With that first hurdle crossed, Jane felt more confident about how to handle the meeting to come.

WHAT WAS IN PLAY:

- Approach—knowing his preferred learning methods from previous meetings, i.e., that he is more kinesthetic, RACI, and his interests and motivation
- Behaviour—opposite behaviour, facial expressions
- Conversation—tone of voice and use of curious question based on interest

SCENARIO 3: PASSING MONKEYS

Engaged leaders coach people. An ongoing challenge is developing someone who has a lot of talent but—as most of us do—has a few things that will hold them back. The engaged leader gains more sustainable influence by coaching and empowering his team to make better use of their time and talents than jumping into every task himself or telling them what to do.

Paula is Miguel's boss and recognises Miguel's potential as a leader; he's positive and motivated. The team respects his opinion and experience, and he's supportive and empathetic to colleagues. When it comes to solving problems, however, he hesitates. Paula has always appreciated Miguel's willingness to ask for help when he needs it and had considered it a sign of humility. Since she promoted him to team leader, however, she noticed that he was almost too good at asking for help. He passes monkeys to Paula, coming to her with the smallest of problems and leaving them for her to solve. He seems to consider asking for support a form of collaboration or delegation. Paula wants to be a supportive leader and mentor, but she also wants Miguel to bring potential solutions to her rather than drop his problems on her doorstep.

Paula hears Miguel's footsteps in the hallway and begins to feel agitated. She takes a deep breath. Paula kept her door open for emergencies, but Miguel's dropping in unannounced frequently interrupted her train of thought when she was working on detailed memos. She mentally reminds herself to close her door when she's doing deep work.

Paula had promoted Miguel to project leader within her team to lead the new project, which was given to Paula's department by the CEO, on improving procurement compliance with suppliers. Not only would it lessen her load, but it would be an opportunity for Miguel to demonstrate his leadership skills. Some days, however, it feels like she has to do both their jobs. Paula wants Miguel to think for himself and use the available resources to come up with options to solve the issues he finds himself, not only to save her time but more importantly, to develop his skills as a problem-solver and upcoming leader.

Paula is conscious not to pass monkeys up to her own leader. Early on, Paula learned the two-solution rule from her boss: for every problem she has, she should bring two solutions, her preferred solution and one other solution that she thinks might work but may have some risks or issues associated with it. She knows she can then discuss with her leader how to choose between the two options and determine if her preferred option is the best option. She's going to pass this approach onto Miguel.

Paula knows she needs to change her own behaviour for Miguel to change his.

She decides to take advantage of the current interruption for a coaching opportunity. She wants to accomplish two things: manage Miguel's behaviour of interrupting and have a conversation about the two-solution rule. Paula stands up just as Miguel reaches the threshold of her office, his hand raised as if to say, 'Hi, here I am,' and he puts a step forward through the open door. Paula quickly scans her calendar for an appointment she could offer him. As soon as Miguel starts to speak, saying, 'Hi, Paula, could you tell me how I fix this problem I have with...' Paula politely interrupts him with an empathic tone, smiling face and open-armed body language, and then tells him that this is not a good time for her and gives him an appointment time with a normal meeting room booking to signal her office was not the best place for this conversation. She then asks him if he could come prepared with the issue and to bring two solutions to the meeting, which they can discuss to decide which was the best one. Miguel looks a little surprised and says he understands, apologises for the interruption and agrees to a date and time before heading back to his desk.

By standing up, Paula quite naturally interrupted Miguel's expectation that they would sit and discuss his 'monkey' on his demand. She also gave him an appointment and set the expectation for the next meeting. Paula is pleased that she took action. Miguel is motivated to grow as a leader, and part of Paula's leadership responsibilities is to help him grow. In their meeting, she'll affirm Miguel as the expert in his subject and explore the two suggested solutions for each problem.

Paula sees Miguel's strengths and development areas. He's got a lot of positive qualities. Paula uses his ABC to coach Miguel on his ABC.

WHAT WAS IN PLAY:

- Approach—analysis of his behaviour, planning her response and what she will say, i.e., conversation
- Behaviour—standing to greet the interruption, empathic body language, changing the arena to a different room next time
- Conversation—polite interrupting, coaching preparation for next meeting, offering an alternative meeting, asking not telling to come prepared

SCENARIO 4: THE STAKEHOLDERS MEETING

In meetings with stakeholders, often you're presenting a case or project update, or you're trying to harness approval, buy-in, additional support, or resources from the stakeholder. By their nature, stakeholders tend to be in a more powerful position, having authority or mandate. As the name implies, stakeholders have an invested interest in what you're working on, and when you meet with them, you want to speak to their interest as quickly as possible whilst keeping focused on your purpose. If you have multiple stakeholders, the task is even more challenging in trying to address multiple interests that may not be aligned between them, nor collectively aligned with your primary purpose. The key lies in knowing your stakeholders beyond title and mandate, but also interests and personality.

Perhaps Eric's introverted nature was the secret to his

success. Because Eric was both a senior executive and influential in the organisation, people would want to align with him and grasp an opportunity to share their thoughts and ideas with him. Eric would engage with the person, say what he needed to, make the person feel seen, and then quickly disappear. A 'hit-and-run' style. He had no time, interest, nor inclination for small talk. He hated it and was visibly awkward in spontaneous encounters. He wanted the facts he needed to make a decision, and then he got the job done. Despite Eric's leadership skills in terms of being clear in direction and delivering good financial results, he wasn't able to sustain social interaction for an expected length of time. Eric is a reminder that not all leaders are extroverts exuding charismatic charm or comfortable taking centre stage, who bring out the best in other people. Some leaders reached their position because they delivered business results, and the people below them develop into effective leaders themselves in spite of, not because of, them.

Farah is a talented upcoming leader who's eager to move up through the organisation. She was given a project to present to Eric and is keen to make a good impression. She wants to build a relationship with Eric because she sees him as someone who might be a good mentor or ambassador for her in the future. She wants to present the project to Eric to build a sustainable relationship with Eric and leave a good impression.

Before the meeting, Farah did her research about Eric and learned he has a low threshold for all of that small talk. Lyle, the junior lead on the project, was completing the room prep, plugging in the PCs when Eric, who was on the video screen, walked in and sat down. From outside the conference room, Farah could see Lyle was making small talk, asking how his weekend was and had he planned his summer vacation. She imagined he was attempting to build an alliance as he was a little in awe of Eric, but his attempt went on too long and had the opposite effect.

Eric began shuffling a bit in his chair and tried to inadvertently look at his wristwatch, answering monosyllabically. Lyle didn't pick up on the context clues and continued the small talk, to which Eric responded curtly, saying that he was very happy to meet the team and he was needing to rush to another meeting straight after this one. He looked uncomfortable and restless. He was gracious and polite, but his message was clearly 'Let's move on.'

Farah, because she'd done her homework on her key stakeholders, knew Eric's style and easily noticed Eric's discomfort. Although Lyle was still plugging in the last of the computers, she walked into the conference room and leant over to Lyle and gently touched Lyle's arm to catch his attention, looked at him, smiled and then called the meeting to order with a firm statement that acknowledged everyone's busy calendars. She sat upright and directly across from the video screen to be sure Eric could see her fully and clearly and to communicate she had control of the meeting and then asked Eric if he wanted to address anything in particular or in addition to the meeting's topic and then moved directly into the first item on the agenda.

Farah skilfully interrupted the small talk without offending anyone. She deferred to Eric's authority by asking if he had questions or something to discuss other than the scheduled agenda. By doing so, Farah had an opportunity to further gain information on Eric's context, priorities and needs. She acknowledged his time and interest to move on to the topic at hand. Everyone focused and the meeting began.

WHAT WAS IN PLAY:

- Approach—stakeholder analysis, interests, presentation planning
- Behaviour—touching gently to interrupt, calling the meeting to order, body language and seating in relation to the video screen
- Conversation—interrupting, limiting small talk, straight to core issues

SCENARIO 5: THE DIFFICULT CONVERSATION

Difficult conversations can vary from delivering unpleasant feedback, for example, to a team member with poor performance, to full-blown conflict, where the leader plays an active or mediator role. Difficult conversations can still result in win-win outcomes with appropriate planning and well-chosen words and behaviours.

Akbal noted Olivia's talent from her first interview. He also noted her ambition. Akbal hired Olivia as an account manager, and she expected her tasks to be more external towards clients. Instead, Olivia found the work also involved detailed analysis, written reporting, data mining, and attention to pressured timelines, skills which were neither her strength nor preference. Nonetheless, when she ran into difficulty, she was not keen to admit she needed help. She began taking more frequent sick leave days, which Akbal suspected were stress-based or job-search days as opposed to physical illness.

Akbal sent Olivia an email to set up an appointment without stating any purpose other than a check-in on how she was doing. He consciously chose the small, quiet room with armchairs in a V-shape and a small round coffee table to meet in. Olivia arrived at the meeting defensive from the outset, wondering why she had been called in. Akbal opened the conversation with Socratic questions after small talk about how Olivia felt about her role and what it meant to her to be working on the tasks she had been given. She identified feeling she was on a steep learning curve and that being successful at all times was paramount, she wanted to prove himself to be worthy of promotion. Akbal then moved on to questions he'd prepared based on feedback principles. Akbal outlined what he believed was working—Olivia's skill in building rapport with customers; what he would like to have seen more of—timely, detailed reports; and what success in the role would look like—growth of customer spend based on data mining. Akbal asked Olivia for her reflections on his comments and together, they identified the gap between what had been delivered so far and where improvement was needed.

Olivia admitted that she dislikes the detailed tasks, which arc far from her motivation or preference. She confessed that she's stressed with having to work with numbers and fears making costly mistakes.

Initially, Olivia said no to exploring new roles and tasks, truly believing she'd just stick at it until she got it right even though she was unhappy and stressed. Eventually through Akbal's empathic stance, appealing to what being successful at work means to her and curious questions to elicit tasks she feels she performs best, she opened up to the idea of an alternative role in a different department.

Akbal explained that people perform best when there is a good degree of overlap between preferences and tasks, although understandably, that is impossible to attain 100 per cent of the time. Akbal had prepared both a BATNA and WATNA and suggested another meeting to discuss a new role in another department which would be a better match (BATNA) versus staying in the role at the risk of experiencing more stress (WATNA). In the second meeting, Akbal and Olivia found their ZOPA on a same level role at the same salary within the same business area but in a different department working as a Key Account Manager toward vendors. The collaborative effort resulted in a win-win solution.

WHAT WAS IN PLAY:

- Approach—prepared data, BATNA, WATNA, ZOPA
- Behaviour—empathy, 90-degree seating at a small coffee table
- Conversation—curious and Socratic questioning, Ladder of Inference, feedback, looking for alternative options, agreement and commitment to the result

SCENARIO 6: LEADING CHANGE

When change happens, people will often say, 'I should have been involved. I can't believe they didn't tell me.' Leaders often forget that it's far better to communicate that there's nothing to say than not to communicate at all, leaves space for noisy ghosts as I call them. In the absence of information, people will create their own story of what is happening, which is often far worse than the truth. The engaged leader will acknowledge that management is working behind the scenes and that as soon as there is something to share, it will be shared. Constant dialogue instils trust with the people who will be affected.

The board gave Olav the mandate to review the company's whole performance management structure, specifically compensation and benefits. Their goal is to review performance and reward, including salary, bonuses, and reward packages that will incentivise the employees to deliver more whilst ensuring a stronger financial future for the company. Olav is the HR manager and decides to announce this review process to the organisation because he wants it to be seen as having positive benefits to everyone. He doesn't want the review to be perceived as policing but rather as an opportunity for employees to earn more and receive individual bonuses for hard work, effort and results.

Olav needs to guide a project team who will help him identify the solutions but also communicate the process to the organisation. He needs to bring the correct people into the team and pinpoint the key stakeholders.

Olav uses the RACI tool to determine who needs to be in the group, considering who will be responsible for which tasks (R), who will be accountable (A), who needs to be consulted along the way and on decisions (C), and which stakeholders must simply be kept informed (I). He knows a project of this scope crosses departments and silos and must include human resources, finance, and internal communications as well as legal and the union representatives. He gives due thought to the people and timeline before communicating the process to the organisation. As an engaged leader, he doesn't want to create anxiety or fear in people about potential changes in their base salaries or spur the wrong idea that this is simply the beginning of a reorganisation that will lead to people losing their jobs.

Olav, himself, had been subject to a mismanaged reorganisation where the change was handled poorly, people learned of the change from one day to the next without warning and stakeholders weren't informed, let alone consulted, in advance. In that past circumstance, Olav had been responsible for a large part of the organisational operations, yet he learned about the changes the same day as his people did. They asked relentless questions about why management was making the changes and what it would mean for them. He couldn't answer their questions and was frustrated by his management. He didn't want to repeat those mistakes.

Olav had the project team all work with implementing Kotter's eight steps to change management. The starting point was to create an aligned 'why' story with the board and management team about why the changes were being made, what was in it for the business and for the employees and the consequences of those changes. Once that was created, Olav had to consider how to share it with the organisation. He could send it out by mail, put it on the intranet or simply ask his team to spread the work through their departments. Knowing that there would be a lot of questions that would need answering, and concerns about loss of pay or benefits with a new approach to performance management, he chose to do it in person. He sent out a newsletter outlining the reason for the coming change with a meeting call attached for a town hall meeting where everyone was invited, and he would stand on stage and talk through the reason for the changes and timeline of the project. He knew if he simply resorted to written communication or a prerecorded video, he would be seen as weak and hiding behind the screen, so to speak, avoiding difficult questions. As an engaged leader, he was empathic to the employees needs to have physical access to him to ask and get answers to their concerns.

Ahead of the town hall, Olav ensured his team was fully prepared with likely FAQs and were available on the day to answer questions in the room as they arose. They were briefed to collate all new questions raised in the sessions and add them to the intranet where all employees had access to those in case they were absent at the town hall or simply for future reference. He made it clear to his team that they all answered only those questions that they had prepared answers to and would revert with answers to those they did not—thereby avoiding any impulsive and unconsidered responses that may add to the confusion. He knew that his physical presence would send the signal that he was personally owning and committed to the project and that he and his team were freely available for questions and clarifications. Video streaming the town hall live across locations gave everyone the opportunity to join the session and opening up live chat rooms on the intranet gave everyone an opportunity to ask questions. Locations appointed moderators to post the questions and answers in real time. Such an important change to reward and performance was going to affect everyone and with the potential for great benefits. Olav knew that getting this done the right way was going to be far more successful in the long-term in terms of acceptance from the employees than simply getting it done.

Olav took to the stage well prepared in his presentation. A few key words on the background and timeline, with pictures on his PowerPoint presentation set the backdrop for his speech. He sat sleeves rolled up on his white shirt on a bar stool type chair on the stage. One leg on the floor the other on the rung on the stool itself. Dress and body language open and relaxed conveying a clear message that this is about all of us together (no power suiting or podiums), and that he was involved in the work with them. He looked directly at individual faces in the audience in front of him and addressed the other locations both in his welcome and as he explained the project. His tone soft and empathic, he talked to their likely concerns and provided reassurance and firmed his voice slightly for the project plan and timeline for delivery as he asked for their commitment to the process and outcome. He appealed to their interest in having better bonus rewards and a stronger economy giving better opportunities in the future. He stayed firm in his tone to appeal to their patience and understanding as the changes may take time to implement.

WHAT WAS IN PLAY:

- Approach—stakeholder analysis, RACI, preparation of team and 'why' message through use of Kotter's change tool
- Behaviour—choice of dress and open body language, showing empathy, physical presence in choice of arena, multiple modes of supporting communication—video, chat rooms, newsletter
- Conversation—preparing questions and answers in FAQs and then live chat, varying tone of voice,

empathic and appealing to understanding and commitment

Often large corporations and matrix organisations have business lines that are responsible for delivering core business and process lines that take care of the common competencies required in business. Managing a project across a matrix organisation is a huge demand on a leader's influence without authority. Often the project leader needs the cooperation and collaboration of a number of people who aren't direct reports but provide resources or counsel for the project. The leader must find a way to persuade and influence them to provide the support that he doesn't have the authority or mandate to demand.

ABC comes into its glory in these situations. The engaged leader approaches the situation with thoughtful preparation, enters the room with considered behaviour in body language and position, and uses questions to steer conversations to a win-win negotiation. Whilst relationships are built and strengthened over time, planning the approach, behaviour and conversation is just as important on the fiftieth meeting as the first.

CONCLUSION

Don't confuse presence with influence. Becoming a leader at any level and getting a seat at the table simply isn't enough. It's what you do with it that counts. How you use the space you take is far more important than having the space itself. It's about the reputation you leave behind, the conversations people have after you've left the room, and what's said about you when you're not there. And what if you can't get a seat at the table you'd like? Then find the people that the table listens to and build influencing relationships there. Your PIN Code to success is based on building willing and winning relationships wherever they may be for now or later.

Being a professional expert doesn't make you an effective leader. What you know is of little value if you can't translate its use effectively to others or garner support for your ideas to make a difference. It boils down to being effective in all three aspects of your leadership: leading your team, collaborating laterally with peers and building alliances with senior and external stakeholders. This book doesn't intend to replace the wealth of models and theories to be found in all those leadership books on the top of best-seller bookshelves nor development programs taught by business schools. And neither does it try to teach you your business. Its purpose is to provide the three keys of everyday leadership effectiveness in a simple, memorable and practical framework. Persuasion, Influence and Negotiation—PIN—is what you need to do and your Approach, Behaviour and Conversation—ABC—is how to do it, to have the positive impact you intend to have. Whatever else you learn from a book or a program, you'll need to be able to apply it in practise, and the skills in this book are the way to do that, and the method the simplest way to remember them.

Engaged leaders want every encounter to end on a win-win note. They actively look for their blind spots and seek to learn what is necessary to move the needle on the leadership spectrum closer to engaged and farther from entitled. They are skilled at bringing out the extra mile in people creating winning results. Engaged leaders know that if the people thrive, the business will also thrive.

The Leadership PIN code provides a framework that gets better with practise. Each time you plan your approach, behaviour and conversation, receive feedback and adapt, the further towards engaged leader you'll go. It enables you to translate what you know into your daily leadership. It's about how you get your ideas across, how you engage others, and how you make a lasting, positive impact. It's how you win hearts and minds to create willing and winning engagements.

When you put this book down, what are you going to do now? What action will you take to move the needle towards engaged leader? What are you planning to say to that person you're about to meet or the room you're about to walk into? Check your body language as you close the book and walk toward the door. Think about what you're actually going to say next.

Take a minute right now: what's in your PIN code for the encounter you're about to have?

ACKNOWLEDGEMENTS

To my dearest friends and family—in so many ways you have all unknowingly played your part in me finally writing a book. The process of writing it has taken courage in the face of fear, resilience in the face of adversity, perseverance when the odds are stacking up, integrity in meeting challenges, trust when feeling doubt, humility in self-belief, and greater belief in the power of the universe. Thank you for these life lessons through our treasured relationships all these years.

My darling son, my sunshine, thank you for your patience and cups of tea whilst I have been absorbed in my thoughts in writing. I love you more than any words can capture.

To my marvellous book writing inner circle—this book is really your fault! If you had laughed when I said I was writing a book, it would have fallen at the first hurdle. Jokes aside, I want to share a very special thanks from the bottom of my heart to each of you for your ideas, contributions, cheers of support and unrelenting belief in me and PIN. You said I could, I should and I would...so I did, and you are forever tattooed in my heart and now in the book because of it.

In particular to Lucky and Dia, a huge thank you for taking the time and providing invaluable feedback on the final draft—it truly made all the difference.

A special thank you to Chiara, my personal trainer in many ways, for helping me discover the life-changing link between physical and mental strength—and for your endless skilfull encouragement when it was tested to its limits.

To my colleagues past and present, and clients along the way, thank you for your incredible championing of the Leadership PIN code in presentations, workshops and written drafts—it has been absolutely invaluable and really the catalyst in bringing it to life.

A huge thank you to everyone on the Scribe team who kept me afloat and on track, and whose expert guidance in my book idea is the only reason it actually got written. Special thanks to Rikki for believing in it from the very start, Kacy for her championing support and flexibility, my immensely talented and humble scribe Barbara, and Erin and Cindy for their creativity and patience with the cover design!

To Frank Dick and Bonnie Fetch for inspiring me with their brilliant books and their personal encouragement to dare myself. Thank you so much.

To all the engaged leaders I have ever had the privilege to meet—thank you for influencing me and others to try to reach our full potential whilst also trying to reach yours. You are what the world needs more of everywhere, every day.

ABOUT THE AUTHOR

Whilst my CV verifies where and what I've done and the standard and quality of the teaching or training, it is my experiences, successes, failures, lessons and choices that inform the book and serve as the basis for judgement on whether what I share is valuable to you, the reader. I'd like to believe that I fall more toward the engaged leader end of the spectrum—either leading or not in every moment—and am farther from the entitled leader, because I have neither arrived at being nor am I always, a leader. The needle is never static nor my learning ever done.

Dr Nashater Deu Solheim is the CEO and founder of Progressing Minds AS, and PIN AS. Nashater is an entrepreneurial executive with over twenty-five years of practical business experience in diverse, complex organisations across industries (government UK and Norway, corporate, private and public health, oil and gas). She has held executive leadership positions within international corporations in competence and learning roles and leadership development. She has built her own businesses in management consulting and is the founder of PIN® 'Persuasion, Influence & Negotiation' for businesses and leadership teams.

Today, Nashater is a public speaker on the Leadership PIN Code and a sparring partner and coach for CEOs and senior executives. She has moderated at international conferences and trained competency in strategic thinking and influence for teams. She currently helps businesses with integration challenges across silos, cultures, and mergers and acquisitions. She is an expert negotiator, having studied at the Program on Negotiation at Harvard Law School. With her psychological and negotiation expertise, she has a long track record as an impactful negotiator and conflict mediator.

Earlier in her career, she worked as a civil servant with the Ministry of Defence UK, working with temperamental unsuitability across the military services, neuropsychological assessment in brain injuries, and treating mental health issues, particularly post-traumatic stress disorder.

Nashater trained as a clinical psychologist in 1991 and has held a Doctorate in Clinical and Forensic Psychology from the University of Surrey, UK since 1995. Her doctoral thesis was in the neuropsychology of premeditation in sexual offenders. She has a long-standing interest in personality and its disorders within psychiatry and general population. She is a registered psychologist and practitioner in Norway and a member of the British Psychology Society.

She currently lives in Norway with her teenage son. She enjoys a diverse set of hobbies and interests including ice hockey, opera, Thai boxing, and flamenco. Nashater loves to travel and explore new cultures for their music, dance and food.

FOR MORE INFORMATION

If you're interested in PIN coaching and training programs or becoming a PIN ® Leadership Consultant or Training Partner and having access to our unique expertise and tools for your own organisations or clients of all sizes, in all industries, please send your enquiry to post@progressingminds.com

Dr Nashater Deu Solheim can be contacted directly for public speaking engagements at nashater@progressing minds.com.

CPSIA information can be obtained
at www.ICGtesting.com
Printed in the USA
BVHW031736050321
601770BV00001B/4